# A Thing About Language

# A Thing About Language

Gerald Burns

With a Foreword by
Robert Creeley

■ SOUTHERN ILLINOIS UNIVERSITY PRESS
■ CARBONDALE AND EDWARDSVILLE

Copyright © 1990 by the Board of Trustees,
   Southern Illinois University

Foreword © 1990 by Robert Creeley
All rights reserved
Printed in the United States of America

Edited by William Cahill
Designed by Liz Fett
Production supervised by Natalia Nadraga

Library of Congress Cataloging-in-Publication Data

Burns, Gerald.
   A thing about language.
   (Poetics of the new)
   I. Title. II. Series.
PS3552.U73244T47   1990        814'.54        89-6034

ISBN 0-8093-1528-9

"Mussels" from *Twelve Moons* by Mary Oliver. Copyright © 1977 by
Mary Oliver. First appeared in the *Atlantic Monthly*. By permission of
Little, Brown and Company.

The paper used in this publication meets the minimum requirements of
American National Standard for Information Sciences
—Permanence of Paper for Printed Library Materials, ANSI Z39.48-1984. ⊗

# Contents

# Foreword

Robert Creeley

The comfortably adamant presence of *things* in this attractively various writing is a constant pleasure. An earlier title of the book was *The Prose Object* and one can well understand its emphasis upon the factuality of saying things, the hand or mind-made disposition of whatever it is we presume a product of words to be. The author speaks of himself as "18th-century trained" and makes the significant point that in our present ways of thinking about writing and reading, "Interest and interesting are replaced by attention. . . ." But, as he continues, "qualities without quantification are no damn good ["How to Nonread"]." A world without sound or savor or sight, reflected or otherwise, is so close to unimaginable as to make only a very little difference. So it is that Gerald Burns is constantly attached literally to all that he is aware of, has learned, thought, heard of, or read in a way that makes his place in this book a very engaging one, because he is, as ourselves, *the reader* as well as the writer. The poet Robert Duncan had a useful way of saying, "I can't remember if I wrote it or read it . . ." "It" is agreeable to either.

But it is another sense of this collection I had wanted to begin with, just that it seems to me unique and reassuring at a time when so much discussion of literature has come to depend upon the use and demonstration of an objectifying system—which by no means proposes a story or poem as the substantial "meaning" we might remember. Again it makes sense to emphasize that Burns is one of the great and all but extinct readers, a fact that is distracting to some who would rather he kept his information to himself, as they say, but not to any who enjoy the endlessly proliferating details of one's "Adventures in Reading," as my childhood textbook put it. Such attachments, therefore, prove a sturdy determination here, and there are clear and explicit responses to what is in hand, and much, much quotation of what has stayed in mind as a not to be improved upon instance of making a point. Always this is writing of example, of specific context, of demonstration. Much as Ezra Pound's critical notes were an explicit "how to read," whatever the text or occasion, so too Burns wants to think of the world as a human responsibility—with another echo of Duncan: "Responsibility is the ability to respond."

No doubt his capabilities as a poet have much to do with the way Gerald Burns reads writing. Whoever knows his singular poems, with their intensely packed-in references and their remarkable articulation of consonants, rhythmic echoes, patterns of playful grammar, etc., knows also the resources and the characteristic address of his work:

> Imagine a capsule containing an unpleasant powder floating
>     on the Seine that as
> it passes Notre Dame, on a fluctuating ripple, picks up a
>     reflection of its back parts and dissolves.
> Its vanishing is where we go to, bolus of caring for fairies
>     hiding behind the eucharist,
> buttresses like heat dissipating vanes.

> ("A Chain for Madeleine")

*A Book of Spells* is an excellent introduction to his authority in this respect, and he is clearly a poet who is at the center of contemporary preoccupations in poetry despite his singular art and its resistance to any facile presumption. In short, he is a complexly determined man, as much typographer, clown or magician, as he is the expectable scholar. In other words, he has been "all of the above" and will no doubt prove much else as well.

Here my own purpose has more confinement. I had missed such critical writing as Pound's—it was the pleasure and instruction of my youth, for I loved to be practicably exhorted. I had missed also the intensity of Lawrence's *Studies in Classic American Literature* with its canniness and shrewd advice. I put W. C. Williams's *In the American Grain* and Charles Olson's *Call Me Ishmael* on this same shelf. Finally it was a tone as much as a content, though that in no way reduces its accuracy. It was writing that had an active address, that spoke to me literally, that knew I was there.

Then there was the consummate American Edward Dahlberg, and here there proved to be an initial connection with Gerald Burns, since we had both gone to Dahlberg at a crucial time in our lives. In a recent book (Edward Dahlberg, *The Leafless American,* 1986) we each attempt to pay our respects in the old fashioned manner. It is Gerald who best accomplishes it:

There is no one in New York I can talk to about half as many authors, and he is kind, generous and tolerant

("Afterword: Conversations with Dahlberg")

Whatever we do, at best it proves a company. I delight in that of Mr. Burns.

# Acknowledgments

*The writing of this book was supported in part by a National Endowment for the Arts Creative Writing Fellowship.*

"A Thing About Language for Bernstein" appeared in $L=A=N=G=U=A=G=E$ *13,* 1980 and was reprinted in *The $L=A=N=G=U=A=G=E$ Book,* Southern Illinois University Press, 1984; "The Word and the Work," *Menu 1,* 1985; "For My Atheist Theologians," *Boxcar 1,* 1982; "Bread and Butter Letter," *Boxcar 2,* 1983; "Our Virtual Friend," *Boxcar 1,* 1982; "Heaven as Memorabilia," *Another Chicago Magazine 15,* 1986; "Harps are Crowns" and "The Napkin of Cebes," *Writing 10,* 1984. (These eight pieces were issued as *Aesthetics* from Wowapi Press, 1986.) The review of O'Hara's *Selected Poems* appeared in *Southwest Review,* 1974, of Shapiro's *John Ashbery* in 1979, of the Olson-Creeley *Correspondence* 1 & 2 in 1981. "Homage Fromage" first appeared in *Salt Lick,* 1972; "Intellectual Slither in the *Cantos,"* *Southwest Review,* 1974; "On Lines as Entities," *Boxcar 2,* 1983; "The Current State of Everything," *Another Chicago Magazine 10,* 1984; "A Line Primer," *Issue 3,* 1985; "Context as Device," *Boxcar 2,* 1983; "Two Doz. Rom.," *Issue 3,* 1985; "How to Nonread," *Sulfur 9,* 1984. "Naked Croquet" was issued as a Salt Lick Sampler, 1985. "Scale and Interest" appeared in *Writing 16,* 1986, "The Prose Object" in *Temblor 2,* 1985. "Stepped Indention as a Halfway Measure" is an appendix in *Boccherini's Minuet,* 1981. "How Olson Does Impress" appeared in *Boxcar 2,* 1983. "Magic in Verse—Some Distinctions" appeared in *Temblor 6,* 1987, and "The Physiognomy of Taste" in *Temblor 9,* 1989.

A Thing About Language

# A Thing About Language for Bernstein

Even the dreadful Maritain distinguishes verse covertly logical or rational from verse which, whether for emotional or exploratory reasons, does float free from "development" of the sort taught in French lycees. Bachelard seems to me to have developed the best devices to criticize it. In English we have Davie's syntactical study, and maybe Charles Williams' *Reason and Beauty*. . . .

The trouble, my trouble, comes from the relation of theory to practice, fiery theory and tepid practice. There are ways in which Clark Coolidge is not a savior. Or can I take his collar as celluloid. Or leather, around a wood armature with buckles and straps, perhaps rings. This is for a strong neck, to go through. Inventing it took centuries. Now we find them on the sides of barns, like toilet seats.

My favorite barn, which lately had lions in, was really a garage and had in it, on the workbench the hearth-idol of which was a very good, very heavy vise, in coffee cans and old drawers now open boxes such iron fitments as I found in my farm rounds. They were sometimes useful, especially the metal straps and hasps, bendable in the big vise, with effort. These also, the smaller bits, provided me with nipples for plastic caps in redesigned one-shot pistols for conjuring. In general the pleasure was double: of finding and hoarding, and recognizing a use in a cog plate or pierced metal bracket.

Were these, in the ground, words or syllables. Wire fence, bolts and folded drum stock had been grown into by a tree. Large washers, screwdriver shanks and whole saws were in the ground by it. So the tree defined a junk heap, was a locale, probably on the theory that you had to walk around it anyway. Like, in a way, the habit of tacking up old license plates.

There was charm when the bits were old enough (rusted spark plugs are still boring) and potential utility, and as in a time-game the charm of potential utility. The secret pleasure (recall De Quincey on the pleasure of sliding gold coins) was how pretty (not triste) they were, in cans and boxes, *waiting* in senses to be used but not at attention, not sentimentalized. They helped define a workbench.

This last motion, the move outward from particular spiked or angled, heaped or glass-jarred presences, to make a larger area was very odd because they did not *inhabit* the area, as tools hung over their painted silhouettes do or did. They were not citizens or politics. It is more that the large space *could* be used, walked into as a unity, like a country not thinking of its restaurants. One could, though one never did, greet the space. It could be acknowledged, in a different way from how, turning out a jar of washers or fitments, the pieces not useful would still be greeted or given a value while picked *through* or around and set aside.

Max Picard says if words didn't go out of themselves or refresh themselves *in* things, they would hang around in heaps and impede our movements, like things in a warehouse. That *may* be an argument for reference. One could prefer the warehouse, as one dreams in a surplus-parts store. Will this be sought out or printed—ever be more than *browsing*. And is there, built into some kinds of experiment as result, the utility of browsing only. Please reply.

# The Word and the Work

## 1. DO SCULPTURES REFER?

It is possible to feel giddy confronting the Dallas administrative build-ing with the Henry Moore sculpture in plain sight, itself fronted with a little lake with a giant red ball with an apple-bite removed, on the water, revolving. The large bronze is not absurdly referential—does not even I think refer to Moore sculptures as notion or category (as one might say "the Chevrolet," intending a generic assemblage of qualities). Yet the objects, more or less on a plane, are apposed, as if intended to be alike significant, unless we think of the ball as there to amuse the sculpture. Perhaps in this sense it is possible, as in a hall of Eminent Men, for sculptures to refer to each other. Wax museums will be more of a group.

Anyhow, something about the Moore/ball combine thwarts the aes-thetic attitude or numbs it, as if something skipped over water, a scent lost, and you may, then, think instead of civic expenditure (perhaps as itself an art) devolving on relatively permanent things which will themselves be perceived as expensive, then as durable, then as art. Large company logos outside buildings do this.

In any case the object or thing pictured tends to vanish, down vistas of comparative usages, with values which simply do not relate to each other.

## 2. (GERMANICALLY), DOES REFERENCE SCULPT?

So we can have a new, either corporate or civic, reason for picturing an object, for which my private reference has always been the giant board or tin hotdog over the building selling them. Not to put London signs on ours as a matter of course—I mean no more than that monu-mental identifications can function as a kind of art, if the identification is recognized as generic—a cup *of* tea. Some tea. When I was small, the house I grew up in was kittycorner across the street from a gas station. This was Detroit, and in the forties retail locations gave away things. Some were thin tough board, with slots and tabs to be made into things (like the lovely colored masks of television comedians on cornflakes boxes, same period, with cheeks and noses one bent to insert). One station gave away a red horse with wings, quite cleverly designed with a blocky body and foldaround legs. When you bent the torso, as I recall, the wings flapped.

Now this, though I read the *Wonder Book* and so on, was my only relation to Pegasus that stayed, perhaps for the hand in its construction, or watching the wings move—just a little—when it was done. The legs and hooves were throwaway, dripping from the body as lodge emblems depend from a watchchain (the waistcoat striped, say two shades of gray, and this not remembered but imagined). It did not *seem* to affect my relation to signs, larger but higher, with the same animal.

## 3. AN ANIMAL WITH WINGS

Mobil did not revive the Greek or remake the bat. The thinnest possible sense, of knowing sculptures existed (and were of bodies) may help out, but I think a winged horse has always made sense. Still, since Trammell organized the show, I have been looking differently at the commercial representations, and with more care (even) at the Dallas Institute's front door, which wants a Pegasus on it and has only wooden plugs for an old knocker or device. I think Hawthorne's Pegasus is more like the wooden plugs.

In short I lack the mythic sense, and it tends to attack me as a confusion when *trying* to see the Moore bodies or whatever they are and that red ball, floating so easily on water, together though not an ensemble. Stevens, in an early poem, proved the carriage is part of the princess.

The Moore might have interesting things in it, bodies, microfilm, an old bicycle. The ball can't. Maybe, like that counterfeit Etruscan bronze horse, it's safer not to look inside. I don't think winged horses have insides, as if they are really, like cardboard with tabs, cut out of the air, patent stiffeners rather than things, to help us think such grace in our air—or perhaps the *air,* subtended by those wings, is mythic. That may be the use of recognition in the corporate or Trammell-exhibit totem, that while it exists or is going on or whatever it does, the air is a little different.

# For My Atheist Theologians

In your millions, milieu, for whom journalism is apt instance, known as trees and stones by Indians (the stones may be moved), why is it, *given* any few branches lashed, as if child's work, you do not make a ring of stones and put this on, with a flayed beaver, or a fish (those metal hinged-fish shapes one roasts fish in, is given or sold to roast fish, given or sold). A text may be the branches but criticism is not ever the fish. And the fish, shall I say, is not recognizable, a convention, as obsidian in the path may be, historically, known like pipe-clay, its position first then its use. This is an order of teaching.

The flames (in Michigan, far from obsidian) are thin in the clear day air. We pretend no clothing in particular, are not sketching from life, as one unclad may roast a vertebrate (or a squash), while we watch and maybe draw. The drawing would be a choice, consequent on the clothing, impedimenta, clothing, of paper in pad or masonite clipped. The naked or near-naked person roasts a fish. We may not draw the person, as the ink bottle's writing (over years, mine with a base of clear rubber added, dried) obscures with ink. The event is transient, but may if the drawing is good be revealed a little.

If there are several drawings.

We do not blaze a tree. We thank bound branches, and thicker wood still not hardly blackening stones, and only as cooking proceeds the dirt, few grass stems now short or absent, itself darkens. This duration of an odor, and really more steam than smoke, and the darkening, are cognate. It would take oil to do justice to the heating thing, drawn ink too much a convention like Western landscapes. I am writing this on flat land with a pen with a little bit of writing on it, as there might not on a pen holder but a patent point for drawing be writing on. None of this may be adjusted.

How it takes the mind to imagine a gift of branches (which are critical prose) as not having to be superbly wound, withied, but only enough to keep them near enough for mutual heat, you see, to propagate. Reading is no conflagration, metaphor the going back to how a thing blackens. All this, from knowing where to find it before knowing what it is, is description. Binding branches describes them, describe as kinder than define. My life is a series of events.

Movements, movement, may be less than this. I want to be back at the flame, so pale lemon does not apply and would have to be imported (say, Ponge's soap in a gift crate), want to be attending, while another who may be unclad attends the fish. I have eaten, lately, fowl. Tinned fish has words on. We are back before print. But if I had a paper, pen, I would draw, not write.

That the fish warms is not dramatic. That the stones warm is dramatic. Entrails, fur or scales, bones if we are not nomadic, go to the ashes after, a mixture not much thought about. Establishing a gesture—washing a plate, drawing a squatting being—is for itself. Ceremony is ceremonially defined. That obsidian can be a mirror, for instance, makes a mirror which can be looked at. The mirror in (say) Tortoni's, where a woman eats a plum, is another matter. The drawing of the Indian, from photographs and a studio, makes a painting to hang in banks. The ashes were brushwood, critical sentences I have not *given* a function but, confronted with, have escaped from by using. None of this has occurred, which makes these sentences what.

# Bread and Butter Letter

A shock to be eating again, leaved things, broccoli and carrot, small tomato and lettuce in safflower oil, astringent and touch of odorous dressing, meat moulded with rough-cut carrot, bread with butter and cats to be fed first.

Wind outside, around corners, on chimes and forecast, made—a town house for tea, as if to let oneself in through a locked gate. Not that late, but to be felt as late. Wind stirs. The mustard pot holds pens.

Black cat sniff-nibbling my pen end, playing with its cap, well-behaved sleek thing, paw to cap catching the light (black, black) like a bear or reaching chimpanzee. They wake up at night and go whuff. Going through life asking things.

Time is more intimate in a borrowed house. Cats out in the brightness. Rooms have more light, fill with it in some cases, as usual in no relation to the cold, though I am reminded of upper Michigan and varnished pine deadened by grayblue light, the soil outside stiffened with cold and pebbles or flakes, flattened stones (sometimes with striations sideways) to skip across water. Fish inhabiting the water without trouble. But no suggestion of blood-warmth, and a fish taste to the fish as if they resisted heating, or the goo in the scales broke down too fast. Light, anyway, barreling in on split fish, the fins and outer skin too stiff, or on large gray-paper fishhead skulls, the genre ichth.

# Our Virtual Friend

Is the technique of verse (the clustering of stresses inside a line, its length, flowing or jagged vowels and consonants, spaces between verse blocs) of psychological interest? or must psychology restrict itself to "content" and "images"?

Exercise: have good poets read short poems they find psychologically significant and see if psychologists find them significant for the same reasons.

Is having an idea a kind of conduct?

If people didn't eat, but retained the habit of buying cabbages, the political economy of cabbages wouldn't alter. Some poems are more valuable than others—more rereadable, and *intrinsically* better—and the reader is free not to read. This is all of the difference.

This *writers' rights* talk always ruffles my back hair—nobody mentions the worst of it, which depends on two facts: (1) literature is designed to be reread with no diminution of pleasure (that's why it's hard to write, and so much pleasant small-press writing is one-shot, disposable); (2) the reader is free not to read, much less reread (and must retain that freedom). That literature is rereadable suggests that cheap editions of "classics" be available for *whim rebuying,* to speak of firsthand sales only. That whole notion of a classic (shaky, we know from reading Ernst Curtius) here means a consensus of small-press writers and publishers of what the best titles are (is there, yet, a reputable small-press *reprint industry?)* Most small-press folks don't impress me with superior taste—talk shrilly in terms of *more* as a solution. Best of all, if the reader need not read, the writer need not write. If he must, if it's a vocation, he will but (since the reader need not read) who is obliged to support him? Are those obliged to support him obliged to read him?

(If readers have a right to first-rate literature, which writers are obliged to provide it?) The terms of obligation don't work here, are inappropriate.

**8**

Joyce, for a languageless generation, *was* our France.

"The modern artist shrinks from the last word, because he feels the inadequacy of all words—a feeling which we may say was never experienced by man before Gothic times." Hauser (on unfinished cathedrals), *The Social History of Art.*

"Ingres has left us, in one of his least attractive drawings, a likeness of the Count . . . ; but while relishing his air of ineffable conceit, we must remember that this fool was responsible for the semi-starvation of practically all the greatest artists of his day. This excuses the arrogance and toughness of Courbet, whose check shirt and stubby pipe were the only possible answer to the Count of Nieuwerkerke's frock-coat, cameo tie-pin and exquisitely pomaded beard." Kenneth Clark, *Landscape into Art.*

I've had to say in print or nearly that the common small-press combination of carelessness and semiliteracy has produced, in our day (*much* more severely than, say, MS-circulation-tradition in Donne's time) the *conventions* of (1) the *approximate text,* which issues from the writer even as an approximation, since he or she is used to not spelling well and being above galleys, and (2) a complicated set of simplicities imposed on verse and prose so composed—for instance the avoidance of potential homonyms, deliberate suppression of there/their/they're roughies, the despination (is it) of sentence-wholes, from each word being a source of insecurity—you can't *trust* the little parts to carry a very large or metasentence meaning. These two collaborate *with* the expectable built-in failsafe countermove: that what is written depends on *recognition* (I'd almost make this (3)), of subject *and* statement, hence nothing wholly, radically, unexpected or difficult is essayed. If it were essayed, there would be no guarantee that multiple readings producing differences aren't equivalent events. Which produces (4), the unacknowledged convention that the texts are not really to be read over again—like flashy cold museum art, meant for glance and nod, the text as visit.

I look at a regional publication, *Hard Row to Hoe,* Roxy Gordon's voice in his chat, poets and records (why not and basketball?) and news of dustbowl novels. Flynn J. Ell: "There are people who love structure in poetry. I don't." This is much more graceful than be kind to Indians, but a whiff of Worker as Consumer. Buys records.
Art is a gift which is given. These, verse in the breaks of lyric, songs

as dishearteningly printed on the backs of jackets. One is not obliged to invent a different pie. Recognition holds here, lives under the pastry like blackbirds. The blackmail is that one is polite to lives, how could one, not. I think the one gift perverts the other, and it is odd these writers want their lives *read*.

As one might fill a buffalo with strong rods and plaster. I've had fierce arguments about whether dioramas are defensible. I like them.

I don't know if rural or trudging lives are honest that way; there is a confusion of expression and describe. Such *charm* in Gissing, remembering the garret and no coal. It would make a diorama. That's the problem: they're a waxworks. With all the *popular* charm. The art I care about is likely to be Vincent Price in his wheelchair.

There is no way to decide *by rule* between the fructifying, barely transliterable grunts in Ledbetter's "Bourgeois Blues" and a misspelled word, record of an accident (or mere divergence). But to make everything performance taps that energy too easily. I guess there is now performance sculpture.

Verse is a more proletarian art because less expensive. The disproof of this is recorded song reperformed on the street. The folk art is song, dance, costume. If repressed by gender, quilts, made from scraps as words are taken to be. Song holds the grunts between words.

It is an accident, felt as an accident, that street poets can in fact write it down. It's *hard* to think of tape recorders here. The electric medium is like water made a medium by the faucet (for some reason plumbing is not the medium.) Mouthing these things. Could one *slur* a typewriter.


What I don't understand is the market, that it exists at all, as if alternative restaurants. What myth supports it? Not that the *best* writing may be found here. To be eating or reading a thing others condemn. People who have not eaten kiwi fruit. Any small press is exotic. We are doing it, you will find us like you is recognition again. You need not have read much? need not *fear for* your taste. People came by and I skimped them because I was trying to think this. Is there a clinging or comforting—yes, to a well-made pressbook, *Songs for Gaia* or Hamady's Creeley. Books more cheaply produced sell me *lives,* as if stating experience rendered it. Can one buy statement? Why would one? This is always described as buying the poet's experience. We blur the distinction and buy the blur. *Break Even* as the title for a magazine. The game (anyway) of inventing band names. The shared atrocity.


The pages are luminous paint. The book is read in the dark.

The verse is not the record of work, it is work. And as such, as my labor, is beyond price as a pie is beyond price and a thing to be near and given a piece of. We are (are we?) all for selling and sale and so on. The book touched is bought like the fruit, better for the hand than a framed thing. Buying records is not as definitive as buying an onion; the record is more generic. Roses haven't names either. This marginal business, giving each other cigarettes, buying each other drinks; one drinks company. I read poems (or look at pictures) by myself. The act of judging is as if not social. No, if I now reach my hand out to you through this page, are you not disgusted? It is comedy, to break through the window flying, remove the wig (stand up, the vaudeville couple who dance, her legs are his arms).

Barbara Smith says it's virtual utterance, in *Poetic Closure*. Well, Whitman, in that Ferry poem I find dull, talks to me the reader who comes after him. Say I allow him that he has foreseen me. So what?

My idea of a good time is a troll under a bridge, and it doesn't matter if I am the troll or know it's there. My presence in a poem I read is like that. The myth is placement. How I came across the book, a life in secondhand shops, or typeset it and get it back (always different) printed, is not even there when I'm holding the book, touching it. When I've sold or given away a book I miss, I miss the physical book. This is how a book is like a vegetable I buy, though reading isn't cooking or eating. Commodity thinkers always forget the energy I put into it, my work, reading my work—or—yours. I try to spend less energy reading theirs, give the arguments a halo of attention.

The angel in Milton, when he argues, is less real. Lamb wonders if there is reading in heaven. This is not *quite* like asking has my dog a soul because reading, like ideation, is a kind of conduct.

# Heaven as Memorabilia

There are rules. El Greco madonnas stand on cobbles that are cherub heads, pearly or blown glass, almost featureless, and this is something about heaven or minor spirits, that or those which inhabit. A chorus has no features. (Angels turned away from us have long noses, to be visible high up.) Heaven is not on earth the way the Marxists say. It's more like Jimenez' donkey, a well or mad boy to be thought about, the crude Adam and Eve on the Andersons' downstairs toilet, leaves more important to be in place than fig, but that importance convention like epaulets on lead soldiers. I'd rather, the tattered banner says, framed, pay taxes than be ruled by the Axis, and what is meant is partly the arrow or spear point and cord, like more immediate emblems in house windows.

One doesn't know enough. For me it shows as, saying something in the air, absently, it's she I address. I saw her pat a guitar once, to comfort it. When I touch an occasional chair back it's to touch her doing that. There is no strength in numbers for that phalanx. It does seem to me to make animals and objects more themselves. This does not extend to the cherry in the bourbon in Lowell's late poem. Too much *in* his control yet simply an object of desire.

That desirables stand clear, on massed translucent heads (what *would* be our relation to cherubs in bulk) as if ground is transparent to grace, or as if density is what persons are, is hardly *signified* by this altarpiece.

Angels in green, Saint Luke ditto—lists aren't it or heads nearly luminous from drybrush, as if hard under like billiard balls—it isn't a face or manner become habitual. That they are in full being, are important, is from an office having been accepted.

Kierkegaard hopes the modern saint might have no marks. Hillman, watching the man ask has your heart been touched by Christ, wonders if one's transplant . . . Saint Peter's eyes are more carefully done than prints suggest, the hands important though sloppy as Hals's. We don't really love cloth, it says. George Borrow renders the awkwardness of people coming together, reacting to each other. Earthy angels with black shadows, monumental dead Christs. I do not belong *in* these paintings.

**12**

So home is not to stand on opal infant heads. Tonight was fried oysters—a very odd shape indeed. Smoked ones in flat cans are dates. These like his cupids.

Desire has no place to stand. Vapor is substantial in order to be decorative. Chariots rumble into the Red Sea, a wrong move in a game, but the large viola da gamba is uplifted. Heaven is *like* the carts we see.

So it need not be idolatry to be fond of a body not pastel. Lowell's "Unwanted" beats the poem on Vermeer. Madonnas are not madonnas any more than sheep (with hilted swords through) are *pictures* of sheep. It is abstract, not Borrow's painted statue for which one weeps. The fact that it is art, for instance, is very secondary.

To what does one turn. That is it or often it in religious pictures, and in El Greco the condition of sainthood is an axis. I can't help but think, corruptly, that we are past evangelism (only an interesting remark if you find it horrible) and that believers must, properly, be ashamed of belief.

That our painted saints be loaves of bread. Bicycles in the vestry, in the monstrance bottle caps. The art of sainthood then will be a kind of taste, the opposite of display. Sebastian, disconcerted by arrows, becomes a figure study, then what. John with his reed cross—well, the *business* of that altarpiece, recognizing, as if you recognize a prophet by reading H. L. A. Hart.

To be standing on all those cherubs, like Chardin, like tapioca.

# Harps are Crowns

"And the Aeolian harp is, after all, the perfect image of negative capability." J. B. Beer, *Coleridge the Visionary*. I'm not so sure. There's a great deal of aggressivity in a working poet's negative capability—kinds of knowing when to grab, or an assent when the water level falls and the catch is there, not to mention knowing when to kick in with it.

It's as if a low overhead on this one. One could start "Wittgenstein got beat up in thickets" in the earlier one, Auden, public sound (at least admissive, permissive), not here. The savagery of conveying information, painting the canoe. Our fish get very fat, a shape like babies or spinous softball. This poem propagates in the following manner (these done *as poems* are now always untrue.

"I am that I am," says Shakespeare. "I am what I am," says Swift.

Manet's picture, pulling the purples to green, of a lion hunter in the (French) wood. Maybe one should think of Rembrandt and Rouault, the late one of the tribal people behind the table. This is a knife, this stroke his crown (the sword, paint as a pledge).

Coleridge in "Religious Musings" and "Destiny of Nations" is listening to the meanings (Forth flashing unimaginable day/Wraps in one blaze earth, heaven, and deepest hell), not the sounds—the same as his verse plays. So the first, absolutely first thing to say about the verse is that it's dreadful. As if that Aeolian harp appealed to him one last way, as "music" produced without effort.

His swearing by Bowles is more than gratitude. He'll describe plain plain Crashaw as (combined) "richness of thought and diction." He chose, chooses, to skimp the ear as Wordsworth will. Whence the deafness? thither, poff. An idea of themselves as deliverers.

"Poetry seemed so easy." Frank Swinnerton, *The Georgian Literary Scene*.

Page 79 of Morse's *Wallace Stevens* is I think the first instance of an insect (an ant) getting into a book by offset.

"But it is hard to see how a certain momentary noise can mean an enduring object, by being its name, so that making the noise can mean the object in a genuinely thinking and cognitive manner." John Holloway, *Language and Intelligence.*

He who inserts a comma in "his wife Joan" or "son John" is capable of writing "the House, Beautiful." Margaret Hartley says the comma indicates there's only one wife or son. My objection is to a series—his wife, Joan, and Marcia went to the beach. How many went? Coleridge's argument against comma-and, by the way, is that the comma is already an and.

Just thinking of them, "Ice on the Hudson" and the dull ones in *Day by Day,* the pretty picture of Berryman's MS Dream Song on the back of the biography, H.D.'s head in hers, young like a deco coffeepot, Williams alone in doing such an affectionate book about his mother. A Lowell biography. A cummings. Not intending to read them all, but that last generation sinks into the twenties, though it was seventies. The same illness at ease even of first-rate ones, the doom coming or the triumph of others. Berryman's stanza thins out to "Heart's Needle" octet but doesn't thin out. All I'm saying is there's *pathos* in this, these bound lives.

Alec Waugh, licking the cream off his cat.

Intent, you see. Rodefer at least notices that who you are, the distinction even between reader and writer—assertion, assertion. The assertoric shape only sometimes generates another. Start again; resolutions are musical. And is not like painting (being revised) because the scrape . . . well, *is* always in progress, the constant of a deformed line constant, recast. 1,365 lines achieved quite quickly.

". . . but it is true of an idea of contemporary poetry toward which Day Lewis seemed to aspire, the idea that by using the language of the contemporary world poets would make themselves participants in it, and would thus make their poems actions." Samuel Hynes, *The Auden Generation.*

It is putting increasingly less milk in the tea as the temperature drops. As one keeps track of wine, so an officious waiter is a trial. What are the *points* for, in a Peruvian dish-cup?

". . . but as soon as history limits itself to being a faithful or instructive account of the facts, it is no longer literature." Donald Sutherland, *Gertrude Stein.* Say as if it is the fact that is imagined to blow through the bad poem or even a competent poem. Will thinking about event or occasion or milieu help. This is one way to plot. I don't think experience presents itself as a table from which we choose, and choosing includes quantity. Probably all categories change their meaning applied to subject. Applied is the problem, not subject. The brass fitments on my door and economic decay are subjects if both abide. Beautiful hinges, lovely knobs. My door is hollow.

For days I have seen strings of paper caps on the ground, moist or dry. Today coming back from mailing letters there was one, pale red and quite scruffy, on the very tilted overgrown sidewalk. With the usual fat pieshape cement fragment, as if a rock.

"However, it is also the case that products directed at relatively small, homogeneous 'taste cultures' (e.g., hardcore pornography, polkas, martial arts films) tend to be highly conventionalized. Most fans and aficionados of these and other specialized products seem to value predictability rather than the innovation which results from the violation of conventional expectations." Clinton R. Sanders, *Journal of Popular Culture* 16:2.

I like all English books on poetry with titles like *The Somethinged Whuffle.*

> But many days have passed since last my heart
> Was warmed luxuriously by divine Mozart;
>
> —**Keats**

Utterance is not sense.

I am taking lead-pencil underlinings out of a Collingwood. Stafford has a poem addressed to a student's handwriting, the pressure, what perhaps admirable emotion behind maybe shabby words. What is meant by underlining so fierce the print is covered. And are these lines the Aeolian harp through which any text blows.

# The Napkin of Cebes

That one might sit in a room (or walk in a park, with walls) with pictures, and—not and be a writer, or even an observer. Mount an expectably traditional speaker or character, on whom even as a judging being no particular weight lies, except initially as one on whom spectacle registers. Chaucer does more. We are here at the level of anecdote, there were these three doors. Well then, panels, as aristocrats would be reminded there had been gods, beautiful in beautiful materials (as later in Italy clouds were materials) and, for the athletic, contretemps in woods. Sylphs are better than thinnest vines against cream, are heavy enough to be prey, or say hawks and dogs are *intrinsically* more weavable than lutes. A sylph does not weave. In *Dejeuner* they are still, so unsettledly there, woody beings.

They kept out drafts and reminded us, there *is* something rich in brocade, adjacent strokes or kinds of dye, soft sculpture to the eye or define the woods as clothing. How a rabbit may appear. For a human figure being on a tapestry is being a kind of god. None of this, even pictured acts of choosing, conjure an audience. Even there one is not there.

In a walled garden there is a temple. On its walls (it must have walls of a sort, not columns or half-door gazebo) are pictures of gods and people choosing. One inside the garden but outside or inside the temple is "looking" at no particular panel while an invisible narrator writes down what the character or exemplar habitant might be imagined to be told to us as seeing.

A rabbit leaps out of the tapestry, perhaps a few threads still clinging. It has only one eye, from having been a profile. No one sees it has escaped. This animal, though never mentioned in the poem, is an element, like the apple or golden ball for which at any time a maiden may stoop. He said he played as well as ... she said she weaved ... one doesn't ask who they *were*. Being pictured is not the act. In the cloth they are texture. Textile.

## FRANK O'HARA'S *SELECTED POEMS*

Frank O'Hara is one of the nicest bores around. The less of him you read the better he is. So Allen's reduction of the *Collected Poems* to a *Selected* is a gain. A smaller book would be better, and where O'Hara really shines is a poem or two anthologized with strangers. Why is this? An O'Hara poem is fresh, cheerful, and impudent. The line is alive, and he can be funny and affectionate without pose. It's not that he is never serious; when he gets serious he giggles. But a pound of O'Hara makes you wonder how frightful the solemnity is he's always chasing away. It's the reverse of waiting for those presidents carved in rock to grin. Vive la bagatelle. There's nothing worse than Bly or Piercy (or Lowell) being serious, unless it's these magnificently printed happy poems in bulk. Think if Picasso had painted nothing but plates and funny sculptures. Such unrelieved gaiety calls up the sort of *Paradise Loft* he never wrote, full of broken bones and real pain, not these sailings after lunch. They are social and bright, like what technicolor does to New York apartments in clever films. They are nostalgic for the present. He is a gifted writer determined to be trivial, and while his fribble is better than other people's mush or woof, there is that lack in the poems of what one imagines in the man and, lacking, resents.

## DAVID SHAPIRO'S *JOHN ASHBERY:*
## *AN INTRODUCTION TO THE POETRY*

I don't much like John Ashbery, for the whine always there under the line, and for his pretending to live in clock time and then complaining about how dreary it is. And because I've a notion that a poem which grasps its gratuitousness has half a chance, but his grasp it too anecdotally, like O'Hara's. I do like him for prattling on like MacDiarmid's long-line scientific ones, but miss their fiber, and talking out of fullness. He begins situationally and rattles or trudges on, like Olson in his thicket, and even the most human bits (which are of a texture with the rest) reduce to effects, atmospherics. Now and again a *thing* stays, like the theater-box-garden in "A Man of Words," less often a relation. But the garden is a relation. I'm just restless at this assertion of a *sensibility,* the hero as Texturizable, like canned frosting. I stand by my poems, leaning against them slightly for support. I don't know what spatial relation he has to his (our ideal is Jonathan Edwards, riding home with notes pinned to his clothes) but figure in appearance they're like old notes in a spiral tablet ("did I write that?")

So much for John Ashbery, but not *John Ashbery,* one of the Columbia Introductions to modern verse, of which Nitchie on Marianne Moore was the most helpful. "The charm of poetry is its antireferential seriousness"—David Shapiro, who wrote the book, after referring to Derrida (*Of Grammatology*) to shut me up, which he does. Shapiro's technique is similarly French, to refer to present *conditions* to justify current art, forgetting that conditions tend to be merely fashionable, lunch-counter ruins shored up against the art thing. He goes on to defend Ashbery's choice of Parmigianino for the long one by saying we're all Mannerists. One senses, reading that poem ("Self-Portrait in a Convex Mirror") that Ashbery exploits that painter's self-portrait as a way into considering *classical* art (as not for us, from the high finish and self-enclosedness) and one's own life (in New York, surrounded by critics) as perhaps rounded but not a made thing one can slide into like a bath. Now I'm doing it. Shapiro: "Because our poetry now must be a self-portrait of poetry in the most shattering of mirrors. Because poetry can no longer rely on simple releasing speech, but must rely on the most complex *re-writing* of releasing speech."

Whatever poetry can no longer do, the presumption is that John Ashbery is no longer doing it. Yet when I read him in bulk he reminds me of Pope—*not* as wit or fopling, but as knowing how to go on so that one line becomes a hundred. He has a hundred ways of doing that, seven-beat lines, hurling himself down a page, or chewing each line twenty times, and that seems a more professional concern in him than any *particular* nuances he may trap. "There is no way to avoid connoisseurship in these matters." Wordsworth's burthen is Keats's burden (I've been reading Mary Warnock's *Imagination.)* They both had notions about how imagination can show us what's real, and tackled the problem of constructing long poems that aren't Milton or Shakespeare. I glean as it were from Shapiro the notion that life in New York is so devastating that verse now is dadoes cut in our privacies. He proceeds to misspell C. S. Peirce. What is odd in this book is that all his illustrations, comparisons, come from the arts, as if his mind were stocked with coffee-table books. Yet the relish is charming, and wouldn't be there without the breezy gloss of what seems to have been a high-speed as well as high-pressure education.

A good but not concert quality viola da gamba will cost you about twelve hundred dollars. I begin to miss that kind of information in Ashbery, not that any fact is arcane; the things Shapiro knows are never of that kind. I don't know. Not to be nostalgic for William Carlos Williams, but *can* one say those poems, the snapshots of workers with lunch pails, man-sized sheets of paper in the street, could not or should not be written now? Reading about Ashbery makes me feel provincial in a bad sense, as if keeping up with the *topical* French were important. A mind in love with meaning will be sated *and* thwarted by Williams's "The Term." That may be too easy a way to be thwarted now, and Williams (in the twenties) will have sounded like Shapiro now. Now that I think of it, Williams referred to a number of the same authorities.

Having finished Shapiro's book, where am I? I have sampled, from his constant habit of quoting lines I don't find very quotable, more Ashbery than I'd have patience for. Both Ashbery *and* Shapiro seem to me jumping-up-and-down sort of people (Dahlberg's epithet for television); I don't *mind* the subject's shifts, falling through his head like a basement, but the verse comes to a series of stratagems to procure *effects,* ultimately an old-fashioned thing to do (the final simile)—like a doll's house decorated by Vuillard.

### CHARLES OLSON & ROBERT CREELEY: THE COMPLETE CORRESPONDENCE (Vols. 1 and 2)

The last book I remember waiting for this long is Ellmann's *Joyce.* These two crisp volumes are a similar retrospect, and the hero is more Creeley than Olson—partly from the proportion of his letters, and because his *situation* is more desperate. They wrote each other so much that this first batch creeps through 1950. At the end of it Olson can rest proudly on "In Cold Hell, In Thicket"; Creeley has written "Le Fou." One delight here is to see it so fresh on a page, as it hit us at the start of the Scribner *For Love,* a perfect thing. But Creeley is, then, mostly interested in genuinely innovative short stories. Fitzgerald writes Wolfe that Flaubert leaves out what Zola will come along and put in. "He will say only the things that he alone sees." Creeley, who thinks a lot at this time about Stendhal and Dostoevsky, will do that in verse, do that *to* verse. It's interesting to see how much of his theory at the time comes from prose. It probably had to. But at the end of volume 2 we're *just* at the point where Olson's example as a handler of verse lines (and praise of some of Creeley's, which a reader denying himself hindsight must admire as nearly precognition) is ingested by Creeley and returned as the verse in *The Charm* and (perfect) *A Form of Women,* one of the prettiest first books of verse issued in this country.

What stays, even in volume 1, is first their poverty. It's hard for them to move around—*financially* impossible for them to meet each other. Creeley will complain, and be right to complain, about the cost of stamps, which is 3¢. Applying for a Guggenheim is a joke. And for writers who are that poor, the situation is grisly. Success is *a* piece published in a magazine. Editors live in a world somewhere out of time—Creeley counts five letters plus a submission to one of them, and no answer back. To Olson and Creeley they seem cowardly or uncertain in their own judgment; *Kenyon* accepts a piece, pays for it, and then doesn't really want it. Even in the short stretch these volumes cover it becomes a kind of hazing. Editors are catbirds 120 years before (does anyone read Poe's "Secrets of a Magazine Prison-House"?) but Creeley's response is not Poe's little study of frustration (as if Tolstoi had written a Thurber piece). He wants to see the editors murdered. Lots of pleasant things happened in the fifties but not many people took risks. Even their gender is beleaguered, and you see in these letters the "man-men" cant that's all over Olson's essays of the period, and rightly, since the people they're writing against are writing with parts of parts, fragmented.

They are slowed *down,* by casual editors and poverty, in a period when authors have pretty much bought in to colleges (Frost one of the first Writers in Residence, in Michigan in the twenties) and it's frightening to see these two give themselves jobs the residents and grantors won't see as difficult or interesting. An odd sign of it is these books themselves—edited correspondence is a function of the university press. This one, which as I say we've waited for because we *knew it existed,* comes from one of the great small presses which kept our counter-Eminences in print. It's as if the alternative press begins (like Mussolini's cabal) to duplicate the functions of establishment letters. The Pushcart Prize begins to be an anti-Pulitzer. I like the idea of a renegade Academy of Arts and Sciences (but not enough to start one). The major surprise in these Sparrow volumes is that Olson is so quiet—he's more careful writing to Creeley than to Corman in *Letters for Origin.* Then one is impressed at the clarity of Creeley's analysis of short fiction, and maybe how *much* improvisational jazz mattered to him back then. Olson used dancers, and I suppose Franz Kline's attack to be for him signs, as if time is a something a physical something moves *through.* He's done that, mid-volume, rendering a mood like trapped duration as the branches of "In Cold Hell."

My feeling, reading these two volumes, must be reflexive—not that their situation is still current, but that in spite of grants and tabloid-sized poetry newspapers, even in spite of circuit readings as if every poet came attached to a Red or Blue unit, I see no reason why their desperation need not recur. They sound *alone* in this correspondence, and if Olson were still alive I think they would still sound alone.

# Homage Fromage

An electric apartment is a failure.

Heavy furniture nailed down by wax candles. Chemical red cloth stretched over wood frames, pulped foam. Shape is arbitrary. This has a vague relation to money.

If everyone does this for himself, no bank is made of marble. Hatteras.

Institutions are inhuman as without humor. No rabbit is that stupid. Such prose is pose.

No waffle is splattered with hot wax. The side of his face is funny.

"But it is just anything." No, it is shapelier. But lord, *How to Write* is dreary. As a whole. Johnson on Milton. Blake doing an epic Milton a delicious idea. But the verse.

A jaundiced time. Nothing eats like it sleeps. Horses could be gay. Lay the banjo on my knee and. Cook the candle after. My skull is next to a wax cube that smells of lime. I did not choose it, preferring bee scent if any. Altar.

My books diminish. Editing is as #$. Let me explain—not the double slashes. Check number fifty-nine for fifty-nine dollars. This is a biscuit.

We are sounding callow. We Can Write. As if it were 1940 in this country. Which it is. She was a Lady Reporter. Clutch the purse typely. It was as if one could hold the presses. Niagara. Dim film was clear. Gertrude, Gertrude, you loved the media, from a far. This will be as. "They did not leave Texas all together but they all left Texas." That is from *Ida*.

One is not in Texas until one can think of a pig just disappearing down the road. That road is Texas.

It was to be as if one were to think of congruence as itself a boxed set of nailed down lines making a box with no sides and no bottom and in it a piece of paper and on it a noun. This is like imagining that quality has quality.

I will prove that this is red. It is.

Let it be an apple on a page in gray and black. You will see it smudged. For sixty years the blackness of red did not irritate. Not in the movies. Her lips are really green. What color was Karloff's face in Frankenstein. Not the one it was, which meant that. Tone points to hue. Make it make up.

Cadaver wolf bat.

If thought were itself capable of expressing itself, it would do so as if it were a label. One of our envelopes is wintergreen. Guess which. Kiss a dog.

No it is not as if it is, but as if as if it is. That is an answer not a solution. Think about money, she said and did. Money is a medium. Dick Foran. Turhan Bey. It troubles me that George Zucco is not knighted. More frightening than Atwill because he looked as if he made more money. Lugosi's triumph was to look as if he needs none. These come to mind because *House of Wax* is playing, and because they come to mind. They filmed what was real. In two dimensions, flat bat.

It is a forties thing to do, this thing. I have a book to fill and will. Will it. Then to point as if it were effort, the effect of effort, labor of labor. We too work. But now take it. Take Van Gogh, wishing he could learn to paint while painting. This then becomes an apple saying look, I try to be an apple, think of me. Me, not VG.

That is a way of labor. Now paint a laborer. You begin to see.

I used to argue with my father that work is not noble. Once he hit me. One does not think of striking a son as work. Strike the lazy son. I deserved it but resent it. That is how I feel about work.

It is not clarity we need she said but force. There is no need for a sentence saying this is true. He had to scrape off the sky. Anecdotes are often factual. Act is in fact. This may be no longer true. Even descriptions need not describe. Take a narrator drunk on that act. What he says is what he does. It is time to describe the hero. Beginning *Chuzzlewit,* avuncularly funny. By courtesy. See him beg.

Yet clarity is powerful. You don't have Johnson's rhythms without his nouns, the mind's awed pause. Club a baby seal to death, another "strong fact" nothing to rhetors for whom any fact is strong. Coercion is mental (Stirner).

What is it to think of a subject, much less think about it. Robert Duncan imagines imitation. Imagines himself imagining. Describes his remembered image of himself as remembered imagining. This is as if to be Merlin under the stone, the man of power ineffectual—if in this case Merlin imagines the stone.

A bent pin is evidence. Anyone can see. But a straight pin is also evidence, that the pin is new or used. Tender Buttons comes from button box.

To the painter as to a reader, the first significant thing about a book is if it's open or shut.

Take the time to think about significance as as much a feeling as the emotive sense of seconding. This is important is qualitative. Is this is true?

Wittgenstein and Vaihinger meet in a bar. They talk. It is significant that this talk could be painted. Alexander at Thermopylae. Dickens in a Bordello.

If the picture were in color the color would matter. Not necessarily if but if. In black & white it would be inferred. Sport cartoons throw a light wash on the faces of black players. Not as if one could not recognize them by line, but as if one might miss a fact. One could instead label them (black) in the caption, but this would not be unconscious. Women are identified in captions.

This is to say more than that what we get is what we see. A culture is more than one person telling each other what's important.

Would it be a lie to say anyone doing this does this. Ornament is that extra, in by that door. A shape which can not be got can be inferred. The quarrel is is this interesting. Right now I should say not. Any more would be confession, like saying I wrote this when I was blind. We waver between lecture & address, Martineau (male). The question of gender begins to be almost interesting when it is irrelevant. To have is not to hold.

This is a man weaving. Weave weave. He does not move. The tree does not bend. The cottage rests, Landor in ink. We learn the moves.

Take the little lines that express celerity. Puff, whoosh. Comic books like mummies are mythic. A school cares to pretend these signals are signs. The cardboard hotdog is recognizable. One does not know what to do with a marble. Base. Ball. Card.

Trammell House of Trammell your book is finished.
Bob's note is a frankfurter you do not recognize.

A parenthesis goes around, call a fence a girdle. The noise of pouring tea is not French. To me.

Moon.

The tendency is to prefer a kind of criticism. If that hat were another color it would fit but might not match. In the days when watches gloves and rings were made for individuals magicians borrowed them to advantage. Later there was money. Playing cards are an imaginary possession.

What is this like. What does this like. A taste for pictures of moon on the sea. This can be painted.

Anyone can steal the moon who can use it.

Say the sound of giant wings appears in a Doris Day film. Appears and goes away.

Zucco's Quetzalcoatl, otherwise only Mexican films with Aztec mummies. Yesterday a color Zorro, dubbed from Spanish, that plot as Pimpernel. Lace cuffs and the suspiciously athletic coward. Tamiroff's feet.

Nothing that a map does is a drawing. A map can be in different ink. A drawing transposed is another drawing. The map humbles itself to terrain. The drawing celebrates the model, and she disappears.
Take the Potato Eaters, not people but examples. Was this intended? Portraiture is in a peculiar relation to particularity, Rembrandt's painted carcase not a but this. Soutine's birds. The this has *become* paint.
I am always irritated by pictures that point out.
It may be better if people never dressed like that at all. Horse anatomy changes as painting changes. There is a Degas bronze ballerina, creased stockings, cloth buttons, with a real lace skirt. I have been as fascinated before. Years ago in Detroit, a medical supply house. (Used) bronze bookend—bronze books stacked with a skull on top, the skull painted skull-color in paint age had yellowed & flaked. This was to me a perfect thing. As it could not have been new. As the bronze looked like book-leather (the pages *may* have been white), the skull

well modeled. A tasteless felicity I should have bought. The Degas was like that.

Senseless to put Moon by itself; the ref is to eec's parenthesis (of course) and also to say moon like everybody else. How is it that Spring & All's wretched prose has such a pretty couple of poems in it? I am now making tea, not like Proust like me. He would put that in & say it was life, whereas it is provable that our poems are better art. Ask the one who stays in Texas how he does it.

I mean the whole point is not whether this or anything is private, any more than if a museum exhibited VG portraits with photos of the models it would be bad taste but interesting even if one were ashamed. The point to me is whether the words are alive & my late trauma is that suddenly the words in *Geography & Plays* are only as interesting as they are. You know how I feel about *How to Write.*

That something is not art can be a proof, but is not interesting. There is always the suspicion that Rembrandt or Gary Snyder could make something of it. And *no* one could have predicted the great WCW object-poems & people-poems until he did them. But one can imagine a culture such that making interesting things dull is the point of art— dull but still art, say draining them of content-interest. Oh, an auto wreck. Well. Well enough.

This is in senses what David did and does with science fiction things, and Creeley with is/that all?

Just some sunflowers in a vase. Only a couple of pears.

We have a throwaway art, and a throwaway throwaway. At least one of these is disposable, perhaps only one is dispensable. The thrill of old baseball cards is to see them as deliberate representation, the bridge to the cardboard frankfurter.

It is like pretending we care what happens to the people in a novel. This is only successful in detective stories and science fiction.

What is a story about. About.

Each along the lines. We pretend a trail. What is that round object with the spring. What is dust. Each may be approximate. Let a bullet not be interesting, and plot its trajectory.

One could write a whole novel about spheres, not anecdotal either. Even Williams mentions how dots make patterns. He should have said nickels.

The dog is eating her rubber banana. The dog is standing over her rubber banana. The dog has left her rubber banana. Good dog.

Kleenex prose dissolves in air. Flashes of light appear strangely. What has burned out. What has arrived.

Perhaps this cannot be done at all. Perhaps I should walk the dog. I once almost had the energy to raise a theory that art is a leash.

If connection is also contingent—mere succession, say, in a block of time—it is not interesting enough. I should say that since the 20s my countrymen need reasons, which is why Stevens titles please & why it's such a tragedy that with the exception of Stein none of our people in Paris could think. Think how wonderful it would be if Pound could think. Eliot. Williams. Maybe Olson, though he can do something rather like thinking, & in *Letters for Origin* inadvertently thinks consecutively. That book is a better novel than most novels.

Befriend an elephant and take him home. What is that to me? Let me tell you why you should care about my dog.

Cause or reason, as I said in "Philosophy in an Old Key" that Haining dropped the line out of & otherwise botched up. It is possible to know the reason for a line but never the cause. Duffer moderns find this an interesting mystery. Professionals know it is as uninteresting as knowing how a magic trick is done. This is not yet a Poe heresy of Effect.
A reason is a cause the mind makes. Today I sold my Hume, damned if I know why. To Gertrude Briggs, for an Olson.

The dog importunes me to play. I put this in because Gertrude Stein whom this is and is not about always wrote about dogs when she got bored. I am not bored, just importuned.
She has a lovely muzzle with a little leaf tongue and agate eyes. She rests her head on her paws, blinking, her equivalent of drumming her fingers. She knows I see her.
Distraction is an interesting category hard to think about. What I had been going to say was that while chucking Hume I want a Vaihinger to bind with my short-form Kant *Critique.*

There, I scratched her chin and she beat my boot with her tail. Communion.

Invent a fable. Once a dog went to the moon. And dug a hole and buried it.

Is this science fiction. No because there is a dog in it, and that is not how science fiction uses dogs. It uses them as observers. Searcy uses them as dogs, like a Dutch picture of food.

All the things I wanted to put in poems but couldn't, like the charming Picasso *Homage à Gertrude,* tempera on wood, lovely throw-away. Angels blowing horns, quite dark, and lettered.

Cold red wine, turning.

My students went on about Letter Prose, not bad for what we have—Olson, Pound.

The Will can be a subject, not what but that I choose to say. Caprice I believe comes from goat, like tragedy, Olson thinks Dante said. What is the point of this?

Who in a book on How to Write would include a chapter on diction. That any word at all can be said is wonderful. But not sufficient for art if there is more than one. If we had had two moons.

The circumstance is a recovery and a count. The count is 13 in a year and the recovery is from a fever. This is the nature of explanation.

The grave opens from below because it is more interesting that way. The child does not know that, and is frightened. The dog is amused.

Porcupines smell of plastic when they are yellow and squeak. Description without explanation.
Whether this is always coy.

They say that dogs are frightened by deathmasks of apes. Would David ask if they are frightened by Bacon's pictures of Blake's, or do I just wish he would. VG sketched others' work but only Blake put Milton in a poem.

A change is to never again say just peaches. This is always wished. The change is that once again and in prose I am writing to audiences. To pretend while doing it not to is coy, and this may be what she meant. This has nothing to do with finding strangers intimate. I think there is an owl in my beard. This is said to someone.

It has a gold line around, and is an envelope to contain spheres which are removed. Geometry is finite, and it came from more than there. Similarly transposition, as these lines are that hand. Similarly. Art is likely/thought is shapely. Cézanne is said to think.

It is a renaissance thought that writers paint. Having failed to write poems with a broad nib I drew pictures for the spring sale.

We make motion amusing when we mime it, but what of miming miming speed, skimming o'er the grain. It is a wish and please.
If I have a glass in my hand it has no shape. It is full and empty. A glass of scotch could be from the bathroom but in fact is silver. If I drink you invent a glass. What color are my eyes.

There is succession, trading Hume for Olson. And the space of logic, the space of cause, both make experiment. These may not be explicit, as effect is the daughter of intention. There is mere this and this, name a list at random, it will sound intended. One reason for rhyme is to look accidental. Then there is the space you fill James will call a sequence. Note that metered prose functions like rhyme, intended but bended. This is about the danger that anything you write is written. It is possible for a painter to be very bored.

A skull and a skull and a skull. This is what Cézanne says, a skull and a skull and a skull. A brass skull is interesting when we mistake decoration. The frankfurter does not *know* it is shapely. We say Cézanne is conscious, he knows what he makes. A pedantry of representation, the wine in. The glass. This is a socket which can be said to take the light thus. It looks as if it reminds us it had an eye in it but this is illusion, as it only appears to be smiling. Your cheekbone madam is a building.

Who said skulls are white under green grass. How we take it is the difference between Housman and science fiction. Lovecraft is the horror of light falling on things it shouldn't.
Cervantes lacks this principle of farce; Yorick to him is funny with flesh on. We can believe Socrates dies but not Quixote.

Gold paint has been a failure. An egg has been removed. A book has been rebound. Two have been exchanged for one, three for three.

Brass and chrome for copper. Red velvet and the green require gold. It was to be a bag, and one of crystal.

A very felt fez, full of gold thimbles. This is to be seen. A blind mouth, a rather black bag a floating pocket. One a fake, two a gimmick, either one a pleasure. These too were invented by others, and the moves are more obvious. I have baked a cake in a hat. Stir it with a stick. Lighter fuel and gunpowder make a little cloud.

Robert-Houdin used a heated wire, five gold coins. Will he make them for me. Five are about many, five make a stack. One of them was a fat man with pointed beard and eyebrows. Another is really Barrows Mussey.

His cups had seams, mine are heavy copper.

I want to be loved for my image alone.

The dog's head is flat. Her paws are crossed. A fact is not an image; she is pretty as a dog. I scratch her ear with the hand that holds the pen. This is not immediate. That the words come at the speed you write is more than a convenience.

Lemon colored pink tastes of strawberry.

Her head is brown but not chocolate.

Illusion is the issue. My skull is in the bookcase looking out. No painting has a point of view; you are looking out but it is not. Surprisingly little is done with mirrors, which can only be used. No penny is a copper etch as etch can. The man with the hollow back always wore a cape. A small French theater is frightening in spite of its good nature. We came indoors when the silver cups were gilt. Sit in this chair. This is a red ball. It is white.

Word, hand written typed printed photographed read. Medium means means, paper is to paint. As.

I have two pictures of Gertrude Stein, one is a photograph.

There is a painting made in 1934 of a girl writing by a table lamp with stacks of notebooks that should be her but may not be. She is crowned with flowers and behind her is a picture. It looks like her but is it. The face is pink and blue and white and black. If it is she remember me.

# Intellectual Slither in the *Cantos*

I still think, after all, that Pound makes himself too safe by removing just one too many coordinates. Even juxtaposing *relations,* the question is does it work for a reader, in the reading, and a simple Wittgensteinian example (Reader X says it works) is *not* enough here—one wants an answer which carries a principle of generality—of general application—with it. And this (in turn) will *not* take the form of "If you absorb the Pound index and live with the *Cantos* for a long time, it pays you back like this." Even Joyce would blush before he'd say there is no such thing as a general reader for *Finnegans Wake*—that *all* its readers were specialists. A book which demands talmudic study must build a defense of that necessity into its general criticism (since the *Divine Comedy,* say, repays any amount of study but can only in metaphoric senses be said to demand it.) But even this is not what I want to mean. It seems to me that Pound, given his old-fashioned art-values, must for his own protection write obscurely to write at all—that his approach to memory, for instance, is hideously dangerous, without being intrinsically interesting. And that the statement that all the ways his work is significant are not enough ways, is *not* "merely" a description of a personal taste. It is obvious to common sense that Pound's work raises with peculiar frequency and immediacy the problem of external expectations-in-general; even being clear enough about what expectations a reader may reasonably bring to the *Cantos* is peculiarly like being clear about (say) Justice. Perhaps a negative judgment on *this aspect* of the *Cantos* would take the following form:

There is not one problem reading the *Cantos* but several, and the "obscurity" (private and elliptical, say) is the least interesting kind of difficulty meant. Any reading of the *Cantos* in anything like bulk that is more than perfunctory forces any reader to be clear about how his expectations in general must be applied or altered, and this problem is in senses *prior* to any list of pleasures that work gives any reader in particular. Further, it is possible to argue (a) that the energy required in settling this metaproblem is ultimately more than the work itself justifies, (b) that Pound, whether knowing this or not is *driven* to present readers with this problem, and (c) that solutions to (a) are *not* mere descriptions of a given reader's private preferences—that crisp solutions to it will be judgments rather than reactions, *even if* the individual reader-decision of where and when to establish or act on a cut-off point may be a reaction rather than a judgment.

But again, more largely, the question becomes: is the above paragraph simpleminded and if so trivial? One has the suspicion that one very gracious justification for a form of criticism that *in form* is more than "merely" subjective ("chemical"—the description of a reaction elevated into a pseudorule, a private law), would depend on arguments like these.

And for the *Cantos,* as for Hemingway's problem with speech as read or heard, perhaps one reader-objection would take the form of a remark that Pound himself raises a problem he will not face, but that he not the reader is responsible for raising—*even if* the problem involves an "external" coordinate.

The *Cantos* announce themselves in reputation and arguably in form as expecting to be taken as giving pleasures analogous in *weight* if not in kind to (say) the hefty kinds of epic. A modern "epic" which in fact is no more than a string of lyrics (the way, say, Croce *read* the *Comedy*—or Pound—choosing for instance to know nothing of classical, medieval or renaissance rhetoric as a complex, formal strategic pleasure) could be taken as cheating at least those nonCrocean readers whose expectations of that form—or forms announcing themselves as analogously pleasing—are consequently richer than the writer's.

Now. Pound of all people will agree with Johnson and all passionate readers, that a book must be readable first. It seems to me that Pound's perceptions of what constitute unreadability eventually took over, and that after a while it was enough for him to be negatively virtuous. Say that if, in a given line in the *Cantos,* it is not given him to be wonderful, it is enough to do no damage. Well, that's true for Dante—but the relation of line to whole is quite different in the *Comedy* (or the *Canterbury Tales)* from the *Cantos,* and I don't buy that Pound's richnesses are equivalently rich, and I argue further that this is *more* than a statement about my *tastes,* that the judgment has to do with how the *Cantos* obviously hopes to be taken, and that this is prior to explicit considerations of blindnesses in Pound, *i.e.* the ways he *doesn't know* he's not like Dante.

Pound, so gloriously fit to translate the *Comedy,* is demonstrably incapable of it. Here he is orchestrating relations and he knows less about *how relations can relate* than anyone. And dismissing Cavalcanti syntax, and "rhetoric," for god's sake, in ways which make clear what the writer who uses "paideuma" in serious art more than anyone *couldn't* see rambling through Greek, Latin, Provençal, French, Italian and English. He looked for sweeties.

That's why I can't take *from him* his dwellings on magic, Eleusis, Woman as Nature or Insight-bearer. Waggoner remarks that Pound is blind to the religious dimension of No plays (as if one were to find Zen *psychologically* interesting). Now Eleusis if you're playing it is lots more than atmosphere—it should scare the pants off you, as *significance,* and that perception of significance *can't be faked.* At least not if you don't see the need to fake it.

So Dante may read Virgil firstly as a T. S. Eliot, recognizing and valuing the inimitable tonic gift. But if it hadn't been done one would say that a Macrobius writing about Eliot would be silly. And the reasons a grown man may admire Virgil as a man of wisdom and intelligence will have to do with syntax and large-scale structure *as this affects significance* (as opposed to the strategy of large-scale disposition directed wholly to *effect* in the stage-set sense). To miss this is to miss *the* reasons why bulky verbal art is business for grown men. I will allow for special cases—and say that effect-writing like Poe's carries its heaviest significances at the level of syntactic energy coupled with an almost religious dedication to clarity, *particularly* when these are bent to relatively trivial purposes.

Dante may admire Virgil's line as a feeling-bearer, but Dante took some trouble to teach himself to think, to give himself, in fact, a Macrobian education in order to write the greatest verse—and Dante will admire that feeling, and the knack of evocative writing, because everything else *about* that writing makes that emotion the richest most human response to something otherwise set up.

It is not "association" in any of the silly senses that makes Pound's structures less rich than Dante's, but memory (including memory of things read) and his relation to it—as if, say, Dante were to say that what is significant about these Virgil lines is that they affect me, and affect me intensely—as if reading were the *effect* of reading, period. That's no position from which to write an epic, *even if* the fact, or quality, or relations, or personal application, or exemplarity, of What Is Remembered (from a life lived and reading read), is largely *the subject of that epic.*

I think this makes a confusion happen in Pound criticism, that shortcircuits the otherwise sensible critical requirement that you handle not what *ought* to work, but what, in the reading, does. Pound mimes, in a line or all through, the effect X has on him, and perhaps leaves it open (too open?) how you're to handle that—how much (a) it would be valuable for you to feel like that—be affected—by that X or its equivalent, and (b) what relation you are to establish—or are *free* to establish—between whatever feeling of "virtual" (or real) significance you perceive in the given parts, and the significance of the work as a whole, *as* art.

My point is that to *raise* (a) by *what you do* and withhold directions *may* be bad art, if you are raising problems it is reasonable to expect you the artist to "solve," in the sense of building in directives the reader is then free to ignore; and that (b) if true of the *Cantos*—and I think it rather obviously is—functions as a subclass of that silliest of all moves in bad art: the hope that writing *about* significants (God, intensities of feeling) will (magically) *make* your work significant—eating the leopard's heart. You can talk about (b) without raising the author's motive, by the way, but probably can't raise (a) without discussing his intelligence. My own feeling is that in terms of (a) Pound is as stupid as Hemingway.

The most interesting question Pound raises is whether it's a good thing to write verse such that, even skimmed, the reading feels like studying. His most damaging influence has been the assumption, by gifted later poets, that this effect is possible and desirable. If anyone reads Pound richly, *without lying,* Christine Brooke-Rose does.* Better, she will show you how. But even she lies in the sense the above complexities were designed to make clear—the most significant thing about the *Cantos,* and the only totally new thing it does as art, is a new directive and if you like a new effect, that reading it must feel like studying it. From Pindar's *Odes* to Stein's *Tender Buttons* you won't find art doing quite that. The point is that *whether you act on that directive or not,* whether you actually choose to study them or merely browse for the pleasure of feeling like one being studying, it will be a cheapness all around if you confuse the miming of a study stance with the presence of the values study is designed to grasp, *even if these values are there in the work*. This is the heart of the leopard Pound asks you to eat, whether he nibbles it himself or not.

Say he asks you to cut corners in ways great art does not, and it doesn't matter if he does it in order to cut those corners himself. That it works doesn't mean that how it works isn't humbug. Pound fudges in ways Dante would hang himself rather than do. It is a very American way of writing but I don't have to like it. I don't mind it in *Moby-Dick,* but it drives me wild when Pound does it—probably because he seems

---

*A ZBC of Ezra Pound* (University of California Press, 1971).

so proud of it. Perhaps it's the Wise Child objection. Our writers feel the need to write a wise, profound book age thirty-odd, and that *has* to be a fiddle. It's as if we can't wait to be Montaigne or Cervantes. But when you get older you should drop the tricks you need at thirty. Pound's immaturity is not to drop the tricks, so even when he's being wise he's not. Pure effect-writing, as such, is always immature—because it vends illusion. Very likely illusion only functions honestly in art as toy or as reinforcement. Poe's value as a writer (and it is enormous) comes from the vitality of rhythm and a ruthless dedication to clarity at every level, including that of method. He reinvented that most charming of ways that mind can seep into art—the idea that strategy may be built into a work as one of the elements to be enjoyed, not that a work should be *about* its principle of operation, but that a writer's being clear about what he is doing while he is doing it is one of the great distancing devices in art, and a pleasantness. What Pound and Eliot got from de Gourmont, they could have got from Poe—all that necessary emphasis on technique. All I say is that this is subverted in Pound for the reasons outlined above. Poe can be very wise, very alive, very human, writing up a puzzle page. Pound can suffer enormously, and even learn from it (though in senses pain is *always* loss.) But assume Pound is even moderately wise. Assume there is wisdom—and judgment—"in" the *Cantos,* without specifying the sense of in. Pound's method makes it impossible to specify simultaneously that sense of "in," and be fairly sure one is not lying. It is always hard to say how value gets "in" a work of art, but with the greatest art it is always possible to begin to box it in. To say that his practice defeats the critical intelligence in just this way is to accuse the *Cantos* of "intellectual slither."

Value "in" the *Cantos,* at any given point through the totality, is variable—*not* because it is in motion, or that the attitude toward it is multiple, but rather in a way that is analogous to the problems you can't solve because you can't recognize the solution when you *do* find it. And while you can say that this is "like life," and so the *Cantos* is mimetic, that too will be a lie, in ways that by now should be fairly clear. The only place value both is and is not there in the same sense is in a value-game ill-played. Art is a value-game, and while some of the values in it can be contemptible, the value *of* it shouldn't be variable, and in the *Cantos* it is.

Practically, the result is not that you don't know how to hold yourself toward it, or how he wants you to hold yourself toward it, but that you can't know both of these at once. Even this is a lie. Say that any successful piece of writing before the *Cantos* did one or the other at any point—contained directives to make one clarity or the other possible. One is responsible for one's own clarities, and if a man in a bar says "I'm going to kill you" it is useful to know how you intend to take it, even if you don't know how he means it—and in fact how you take it may depend on your *not* knowing how he means it, or even on the perception that *he* isn't clear on the point. But a writer must put you in the way of knowing one or the other—of being able to know.

This is still a lie—to be saying "Either he writes for effect or writes what he clearly wants and leaves you to hang"—but here too are clarities. Even the directive "how you use this is up to you" is a directive. Use is the issue. It seems to me that Pound is less clear about his using than he thinks, even though he's clear about what he's *doing* ("clear" allowing for that tranced state in which 5,000 decisions per word go on), and it is this sense of how to *use* what he does that *is* up to the writer—the sense of "use" which means "follow built-in directives at the moment of reading." Even writers like Brooke-Rose who can make Pound terribly rich and terribly clear, and whose writing is good teaching in the sense that it shows the reader how to do this for himself by showing him what rules *are* implicit in the work, finesse the problem at this point—that there is no way they can demonstrate a distinction between rules found "in" the work and inventions laid on it. The phone book can make do for the *I Ching,* admittedly, and the way out is to show a more interesting way to use the phone book. Bad art is like an out-of-date phone book that never was in date. Perhaps it's that Pound "directs" you to read him the way he reads others, but even insight into relation in Pound is not relational. He asks you less to repeat his writing than complete it, in the reading, and suppresses (as Marianne Moore does not, at her most gnomic) the rule whereby you can recognize successful completion. It's as if he wants you to make up part of the rules, but wants credit for all the result. Or say it's like a game with a death penalty.

I think it's obvious that for much of the *Cantos* the directive is: treat any two lines (or half-lines, etc.) as the radicals in a complex ideogram, and hold yourself toward them the way I do toward the latter. Now seeing the root "meanings" *suddenly* is charming, but is not reading as reading (though you could argue he read Provençal, etc., looking for a particular and parallel kind of charm, that has to do in part with the illusion of insight about language, and partly the illusion of insight about *use.)* Like following a Spenglerian insight into a culture-relation. You can't make it do anything but you feel you understand more.

You see the point: the lines present themselves as meaning-bearers in a very peculiar sense—Pound of all people, the one praised for his "ear," is doing something very like "conceptual verse." Take it this way: given his idea of as-if ideogramic conjunction of lines as associated radicals, what happens is that the sensuous reinforcement of sound, pace, tone, etc., will be wholly unsystematically related to the "meaning" of the lines in his prime sense—in a way *quite different* from the normally nonsystematic relations these sensuous qualities have to "significance" in verse. This is a guess. It might be more right to say that insofar as his significants *work* the way he hopes, they work the way these conjoinings work in Donne, Shakespeare, Dante, Milton, and much of the Poundian trappings he thinks essential aren't. Take a Shakespeare section in which the nouns (and maybe verbs) are hammered together with relation-terms, relational directives, but the relations are rather obviously not terribly important to the sense—exist as pegs to hold evocative nouns in a list *disguised* as energetic thought, say. The historical speeches, or some of Donne. It is likely that the "ideogramic method," as a working tool in English verse, has always existed in English verse—and that one reason Pound missed it is his well-known habit of believing logical and rhetorical directives, believing them simply, when he finds them in verse. It is quite easy to demonstrate that he could *not* read Dante, Virgil, Homer, Cavalcanti, etc., *well,* and that what he misses in them is precisely what from inclination reinforced by impatience he avoided giving himself—a minimal awareness of how rhetoric functioned in education for 2,000 years of Western verse. In an important sense Pound was never able to read at all. Most of the large-scale principles built into the greatest verse were invisible to him, which may begin to explain his taste for secondrate writers of dead languages, who perhaps tend to be less systematic in the disposition of their effects.

I have seen no critic mention even in passing what a flatly too-*easy* thing his Odysseus/Tiresias, Circe/Aphrodite, hell-purgatory-heaven gambit *was.* It is an act of desperation of a not terribly inventive mind, and a colossal irreverence in one whose temperament and training made much epic unintelligible, flatly opportunist.

His words are shot through with Barnum. He announces something and it *is* that, but not in the way you're going to take it. It's not that you can't kick, but the effort it takes to frame an objection precisely enough is beyond most of the audience. You become a Pound Critic, every reader his Macrobius, cognitive dissonance sets in and you have no intention of putting in for a refund.

His O/T, C/A, h-p-h trick is a cheap expedient *because* he did not see it as cheap, and perhaps his principal slither is carefully avoiding that insight.

What *are* Pound's credentials, after all, that he can sit down in Elysium? I would argue that one move plus a negative insight constitute his right to be there. The move or invention or manner-of-proceeding ploy is to make a poem in form such that the most casual reader *must* take it seriously; the negative insight occurs within this framework, and consists of not writing badly—not committing the mistakes he saw around him in the teens. The one goes with the other, because cuts of the sort he made in Eliot's poem (at a critical time for the *Cantos)* establish vicious ellipsis as a habit when *about* to write bad lines, as in ways a *substitute* for them (on Pound's own Crocean principles— bad stuff as peanut butter connectives), So that—the bad lines that aren't there become electrified spaces, because of the reader's assumption that they are full of something.

But what about the bad lines that *are there?* as if all the lines that Browning would save if he had taste? It is not enough to say that Pound substitutes the work of excluding (which he understands) for the work of learning how to include (which he does not), in his propaganda and his practice. The fact is that in spite of his sound-gifts, and of course partly because his example has been around for years to build on, and because his roots are thoroughly old-fashioned, no one of genius or even high sense writing now would, if he wrote a line as good as any in the *Pisan Cantos,* be likely to save it.

He sets up rules *so that* if he writes tolerably well it's "great." Art can make energy out of nothing, but *not that way,* not and be readable 700 years later. His true Penelope was American Can.

I think intelligent people who like verse will like Pound, and this makes it easy on his defenders, since his detractors are usually so shabby. But I'm more than tired of the twit young, ranging themselves *with* Pound (seldom with Whitman, never with Poe). I'm tired of his intelligent defenders making things a little too easy for themselves, with only a Waggoner now and then willing to tell the truth about what it's like reading Pound if you don't lie.

I've said all this in much shorter form in my Pound reviews, so will stop. Even I don't know how precisely I meant what I said—how these phrases mean these things—and certainly no reader will. I leave with one line—there is no way Pound can appeal to the Common Man who really is common.

# On Lines as Entities

I recently wrote Donald Hall the most complete description (outside "On Two Kinds of Mixed Measure" in *Boccherini's Minuet)* of the trick seven-beat line I'm using in *A Book of Spells.* You can describe just about any syllable-stress line if you allow a below-line caret for off-syllable beats, the little cupshaped thingy for light stress, plus acute and grave accents. My own is a measure occupying a felt duration, so I've toyed with a double dot (umlaut or diaresis) tucked over two syllables which share a "distributed" stress. Saintsbury, for example, allows the possibility of distribution. But it's too tempting to overuse it. Similarly, Ellis's zero, 1 and 2 notation* for some reason tempts you to listen to whole-line weightings (*and* what Harvey Gross dismisses as "rhetorical stress," the sloshes sense adds)—and for some reason acute and grave accents stay more docilely inside the foot, if it's foot verse you're describing.

I even scanned a section of *Spells* in my letter. Hall wrote back, "For me, as I understand it, this is a scheme which is convenient for you— but I don't call it meter. I would only call meter that which can be reduced to arithmetic with considerable success by someone who is *not-me.* In 'the hand on ball of heel, leg in the air'—how would I as reader know that of the three prepositions in the line, two are counted and one is not? Don't answer. I have no objection to private schemes. . . . But I don't think they are meter."

The line in question is a mixed measure, anomalous by definition and hence perhaps private, though I think my scruffy little system may be taught, at least as a principle of exclusion. A line which Hall's *not-me* would recognize as satisfying my requirements would not be private. What struck me as nearly invidious was his isolation of a single line. Now syllable-stress or "accentual" measure gets along very well considering single lines, though sometimes you have to print two to show where an end-line syllable "really" belongs. But . . . I'd already noticed that my *Spells* lines are hard to enjamb. The measure's delicate

---

*In Joseph Mayor's *Chapters on English Metre,* (AMS Press reprint).

and sense runovers, until lately, were too hard. Here are eleven lines, fairly late:

> The odor from the front air conditioner, strong when
> I come to get my mail: tortillas and deep fat
> a year since the neighbors would throw a cow's head
> over the fence, just bone, for our dogs.
> Menudo in pots, then, served in a language I don't understand
> to relatives, people in what Olson would think of as a polis
> Medrano a word on an old grocery sign, and a politician.
> The family romance: Gosse's father wrote a book
> on elementary microscopy—best on
> the aquarium snail's coiled endless rasp tongue. A
> recording of the sound that would make, a cassette.

If you say to yourself, rather deliberately, "one two three four five six seven," my hope is that each of the above lines occupies just that duration. Of course individually they collapse and are shorter; in my head, having that general length in mind, I'm stretching syllables—including Hall's prepositions—to fit. None of this is admissible under the old rules, and that isn't the point. What matters, it seems to me, is that *if* some sort of quasi-regular "measure" is imposable on current verse on current subjects, without sounding like Whittier, the scansion will almost certainly have to expand in practice to consider several lines at once. The line has hitherto been a horizontal unit—little boxed "feet" in reversible patterns, or a fairly regular number of whacks, maybe with a pause (or some consonant patterning). Or Marianne Moore's counted syllables, like Donne revisited.

I realize given Creeley Snyder Olson and always Pound that my favoring of a regular line at all is counter-Modernist. Do we all swing free. Creeley, in the old days, enjambed more than we thought possible, cutting *into* sense, fuseable. I might think of glass or some such semi-solid that, so cut, filed, crushed, becomes once more opaque. This may be, still, more important than anything I can do with a longer line. And yet and yet. I begin to think that whatever any of us do, the old new-critical injunction that wholes affect parts isn't enough, any more than a study of syntactical cut-throughs (Davie's *Articulate Energy)* is enough, now, to describe how it is that the verse line has become or enforces consideration as a cluster. There *is* a point to make here, but it's delicate.

Middle Creeley:

> seeing, some
> thing, being
> some. A piece

> of cake upon,
> a face, a fact, that
> description like
> as if then.

may now be classical, hard like Gautier—"The Indians want/her to be their queen/because she is such a/lovely color." How these *toy* with sense-units, to be hard.

Middle Olson:

> God, that man, as his acts must, as there is always
> a thing he can do, he can raise himself, he raises
> on a reed he raises his
>
> Or, if it is me, what
> he has to say

These are live lines, whether or not they are, for us, live options. I think *making* the line in that old Yeatsy classroom sense is still nearly the best thing to be about. The best thing is figuring how to get the whole world, nasty little computer calculators, frozen egg rolls, *into* verse by more than reference. Anyone can refer. And rendering something, what Coleridge I'm told called imitating as opposed to copying, seems to demand an absolute revision of the line—one (or one per twelve years) per poet if we're serious like the painters used to be. The drips, washes, thick bits—numbers of things paint does—are like maybe what syntax, nonce end rhyme, ambiguous reference inside the line, and certainly rate (however got at; bad verse has no particular rate as part of its badness) in reference *to* line are. Maybe I'm urging verse paragraphs as the only interesting units for adults, since *lesser* tinkerings now are too easy, anthology material (learned from them, designed for them).

### ADDENDA

. . . otherwise the line is a stackable unit like red plastic crates in box stores. I've tried to think of it as like a fishing line to catch things. Coleridge almost comes to describe it as registering one's excitement in the act of composition.

Lines in set type on a page, in magazines, look plaintive. As if needing something, waifs. The line is never thick enough for its length. The line in a boring poem always looks too workmanlike, a duty screw or freckled kid on cornflakes. A good line—unexpected late Wallace Stevens, Hugh MacDiarmid's in the Hebrides pieces, Prynne's economic poems—has something secret in its construction. Plath's lines have repeating-syllable jokes but are open, and only as taught depend on recognition as propionate. Valéry remembers the effect of Mallarmé lines, as built on a principle of construction he couldn't happen to fathom, which he posed as from what kind of mind would these lines issue. It's a question whether the lines must appear to issue naturally (as in Ginsberg's Sapphics).

Instructions, recipes, descriptions, sermons *may* be prose modes. "Mode" is not fruitful. The Mexicans next door sing fitfully but admirably, drinking. The pauses are rests, not caesurae. A really hip classical caesura broke the *middle* of a polysyllable, Mayor says, so has nothing to do with our cornfed pauses. Why *should* a printed line—be even visually a triumph or admission of defeat. The whole line knows, not each a gesture but each participating in a conscience.

\*   \*   \*

Compromise and perfection. A local painter sent me a watercolor of his Irish hat, in sympathy for what he took as a negative newspaper piece. The drawing is like a child's only with less charm. We artists.

The point at which living an art holds is still the line. Care in Heidegger's sense, a horrible or hideous caring, for water dripping off wet fir trees.

A painter may save color with line, line with color, the double dodge a betrayal (do these loyalty terms, French postwar, still work?) To what is a writer who writes in lines faithful? Jim Haining sent me a *Newsweek* piece about Merrill, whose planchette book I hadn't minded at all, that under the praise quoted some. I was surprised in spite of myself his innovation is in five-beat lines.

"For love—I would/split open your head and put/a candle in/behind the eyes." The wish to institutionalize novelty can be aggressive. Writing a live line is like enacting a law.

That this is difficult to do is provable by melanges, poems made up of several people's, roots and dogs under the trees, everything going to garden, the Briton's Guarantee. Wordsworth thought of them as drowned in small deep lakes.

They are shouting in Mexican outside my window, the voice assured of carrying.

How long a mole goes before turning—or descending to a level not recorded.

Rembrandt's face, Manet with his suppurating leg. It is almost a desire to outdo the world in a kind of fingering recognition.

# The Current State of Everything

The back of this sheet has a silly quiz about sex on it. A long conference table with a big clear carafe and bud iris cut, inserted, ends with this leaf. The stalk and leaf end or float free maybe four inches from the bottom. It is not necessarily passive to sit down and address a subject, still-life landscape, yet the proof, *all* the detail, if now massed would not be massed, be its gradual accumulation even like coming to know a thing. Further, Stein framed rooms in doorways and rendered or let render themselves or it, with charm. Expecting, then, as a feeling-tone allowed while letting poor old vision play, sight even as transposed to crinkle poffle sound or creme caramel as backward tapestry, isn't simple since she wrote, and since she knew that her experiments are always three stages ahead.

Yet there is no out there, no forefront in language, or as if oatmeal paper paste ready to become print, like other print, got to like the FREEWAY ENDS we saw, getting on it. There are no clothes to wear while exploring. The just-good-enough print coming out of California, Hejinian lines or Silliman prose blockettes, will do as like the lady said by subtraction, keeping say middleground nouns unnamed in situations like compotes. Criticism would then be a doily.

These are provisional texts, and a critic is firstly allowed not to bother. Not their improvisational nature but the deliberately inert argon interior (salt grains and follicles, why are there no salt grains and follicles) won't help; it's more like those Kantian imagined volumes filled with imagination as jello, not to be breathed or move from *here* to *there* in. Not that humanized spaces are like those only sloppier. A Magdeburg sphere inside another would as soon fall apart. My stopped bathtub plug floats up. Reading textes made apurpose thwarts European point out the good bits criticism. Proust's nasty bourgeoisie may be lived into, I suppose, though it's a question how much the monocled gent drinking beer (that picture they halved) doesn't make do for the placement oriented narrative, no matter how you imagine placement.

The new geometry may be more a series of tries not trying to render or describing being the act of putting down, and needs more sideways *interests* in the writer, less psychology drained of event (include states as events) and more about haddock or wires running through asbestos

44

not as subject or illustration but because like income tax somewhere one had heard.

The lion in the glass of water is not already drinking. There is no lion in the decanter with its medallion impressed in glass because the stalks leave no room for it, and it is in no direct side light. Which would give you as if pink and blue filters to the water, a gray you could live with. Here on its fuzz of window reflected in polish there's nothing except business, three or three and a half furled or wrapped Folsom points and a bread knife leaf, not really even to be addressed, as if center and piece were two words. A light switch made of bread, or a nose over a mustache so, fumbling over a face, these would please like, the switch flipped, a fountain of water out of the light socket.

# A Line Primer

The fact is when the chips were down Wordsworth was the only one to assimilate ("a sense sublime/Of something far more deeply interfused,") or defuse Milton, as the found books of Cowley's revolutionary poem prove. We've overdone it, Bloom to Bate, fluent mongerings but it is there, photos of Matisse working from the model, maybe nice curlicue blacks but really that whole mode (model or not) of great painter standing there inventing, poisoned and almost deliberately poisoned. And Rivers and people must be come at through that. There is no evasion without pastoral.

Mary Lamb and Dot Wordsworth invalided out. Scraps of paper on the lea. Whatever is a lea. Where the sheep suck. Not to ramble, but a kindness of being beside is better. Cézanne's objects described by Badt, compossible.

"But the phrase most pertinent to our chief concern states that meter 'should be accompanied by the natural language of excitement.' Where this is not the case, the poet has in effect violated the tacit compact between himself and his reader implied by his use of meter in the first place." Emerson Marks, *Coleridge on the Language of Verse*.

That it all must be made one thing is probably true (the desirability of unassimilable bits is a problem). So meter demands a language, in Coleridge, at least heightened in its care for vowels and consonants, and great willingness to breathe thees. But line also and the fact of line (all those notebooks filled, the upset wife, the cold, frost, cheese).

Wrote Wellman today, "As 'constructed discontinuities,' lines are neither speech nor print—like a paradigm meter, say, line breaks are being *compared to* something in an odd way, when they are used."

It isn't just a convention of line; children have to be taught out of line-end pauses. Any step down (not really *down;* you're directed to go back. The index key on a typewriter, Williams's triplets, are different.) The imagined space in which a line goes "forward" isn't away from you. More as if proceeding in an orderly manner. What stops the queue, in line for cheese you get a toy or something.

Firstly a complete line washes back over itself, guaranteeing as a book page printed all at once guarantees that page, as an intended unit, more than typescript.

Like uttering a line very flatly.

Emily's with its rhyme-vowel out, maybe a little heated, the eye rolling maybe. Whitman's six-stroke paradigm, extending as it may but even then feeling it, the shopkeeper tap at the end.

The line is what is felt to *proceed,* not the poem.

> Seest not thilke same Hawthorne studde,
> How bragly it begins to budde,
> And utter his tender head?

This shape demands a complement. Yet no line strictly does, or demands a companion or followup as strict as rhyme is; the rhyme demands rhyme more than a line. This may be what irritates in early Wordsworth blank verse—all those line-end broadvoweled monosyllables, screaming that if rhyme were wanted it could be supplied.

*A* line quoted on a page is too small, though Hopkins's full ones are like Stein's sentences designed to feel like paragraphs. Any rift-loading procedure makes the line more than a line. Found, in print, like a bottle (Moore's title, so always better in itself than the poem) it is a *trace.* Say that a stack of lines, three or more, are trace, vestige, to be looked at coolly like fern or rusty fish-imprint, so long not the thing that it's discounted. What a whole *set* of lines do, starting and restarting, is develop a trace or fossil insistence.

Not vehemence, or buckety cheer, though too much verse quoted at one in prose contexts is Golden Treasury. Psychological or concerned with diction as texture. This is most startling in Dowson.

A line is a sufficient but not a syntactic unit of sense. The motion of the eyes (especially as imagined) is nothing like the motion of the line. When too many of these elements go together you get easy listening or scripts, as in Suckling.

A line is not *given,* it is *recognized.*

You can't paint light, Cézanne said. You do up a self-related model that sits in a frame like a bank. What is called furniture, like the French garniture. He also said the ground color in nature is gray, not to defend bland diction. A "passage" in a picture.

A line is the smallest unit in a poem which might collect dust.

Very short-line poems may be lines; the mind reading down them has a hand cupped, following a rod with gems on. We relax at longer lines, though Swinburne's with a measure that breaks in bits enforce something of that attention, *in the wrong direction,* and his verse fatigues.

If one were to be following a line and then another—the line is the largest unit of meaning which then collapses and regroups.

One speaks lines in Arcadia.

Intolerable mush. A poem without lines could be a stock report. Why aren't there more numbers in poems. Lefthand alignment, without paragraphing, becomes a "column." The critic eye, goes down it like a field. Edges. What energy is it safe to expend. Do we prefer the ragged edge, the rags. A long line wants out.

# Husserl on Vacation

If Husserl (on vacation) were looking at the Cartesian engravings in
*O.ARS*—pineal glands, optic diagrams—he might say they could as
soon be of rural mailboxes if intended as comments on his apposed
quotes. It won't have been fun all that while trying to save something
of Idealism with an irritability in cafes in Leyden, the people inclined
to speak several languages and already looking like photographs. Perhaps it doesn't matter where you lecture.

Not so far from the multiple triangles in Bovillus, for perception
perceived. This skeleton, in a full glass case only a little like a telephone
booth, a part of Husserlian experience though this one's in the Dallas
natural history museum basement—and as erect, floating like Stevens's
Projection B or an illusion gone normal as on its side it would be a
cremation chamber, utters an attention which is ours *by* the jaw spring
so cunning, so academic, and then the cap, top skull sawn through not
coming off (what holds it, and why doesn't the mouth talk). Observe,
gentlemen, the verticality or chestiness of the figure (the floating ribs
attached by rubber, shoulders *bolted* fast) forcing us away, by way of
the Dixie cup neck vertebrae, from the eye sockets which, alone on
my desk. . . . The head as a whole (see Hillman in *Eranos)* has a
different, only psychically summative character. If a human skull had
tusks. This cabinet enclosure, perhaps Victorian in denying the nudity
in a freehanging skeleton, is like a file drawer, container. If the skeleton
were wax, or were dialing.

When the body is displayed, the eyes need not be taken as focusing;
one is less likely to impute feeling to a dessicated whole. So that it will
not help, this anatomy, at the level of philosophy for which this brass
fronted keyhole may be enough, for which a *prepared* skeleton is too
much artifact, no owner or stimulus even to memory.

Paste a photograph of Descartes's face, that nose, that mustache, on
or over the skull. Decoupage a photograph of a stove (or Delacroix's
painting of one, so much a *studio* stove though Descartes's will have
had glazed floral tiles) on the wall behind. In one bony hand (this, the
writing of it, the first atrocity) a book by Descartes. That is too much.

But a full-page engraving or fine-line drawing of our crated skeleton (Dallas, though imagined as Louvain), seen through the glass panels with Descartes's face (*not* merely pasted over) and dimly at pelvic level the stove, is as printed how to be an illustration of a Husserlian model, and one need not add a wax figure of Husserl holding that book open.

# Context as Device

On page 97 of *Purity of Diction in English Verse,* Donald Davie makes the connection he will pursue in *Articulate Energy* between Modernist (post-Symbolist) verse and "syntax":

> To dislocate syntax in the symbolist manner undoubtedly makes possible an unprecedented concentration of one kind of poetic pleasure. Less certainly it may, as certain of its adherents claim, provide for the communication of experiences too tenuous, fugitive or rarefied to be expressed in any of the older ways. On the other hand, it may be doubted whether, unless syntax reappears in our poetry, we can say of it, as Bernard Manning says of Wesley's hymns, that "congregations bred on such stuff should not suffer from flabbiness of thought." For "congregations" read "publics"; and it will be doubtful whether after all Mr. Eliot has purified the language as Dr. Johnson did, or whether any poet in the symbolist tradition can do so. Finally, of course, one cannot avoid the fact that the poet's churches are empty, and the strong suspicion that dislocation of syntax has much to do with it. After all, there is no denying that modern poetry is obscure and that it would be less so if the poets adhered to the syntax of prose.

In spite of the gains for slow-motion reading in the later book (and the two on Pound that come after) this calling it syntax doesn't seem to work; it's like explaining Impressionists as a change of attitude toward line. Hard or soft symbolism, the manifesto and decorative brands, may disrupt syntax proper, inside a sentence, but what's happening is more likely the acceptance of invasive contexts. This is not (quite) layering of meaning as you see it in Joyce, but the poet's being open to other experiences which qualify or even define the experience in question, nub of the meditation. It may not be an "experience," but maybe a theme like "relation." I once wrote paired 21-liners about illustration, the second of a pair a theoretical rewrite of the first, a let's write that poem again, and found that my attention maybe or even the subject tended to float in the space between the two—or at least that that attention we give to subject ended up diffused, sort of spreading over the surface of both poems. Each illustrated the other.

What troubles me now, as purity of diction (that sense of exclusions exercised he found in late eighteenth-century verse) troubled Davie, is the flatness I find in too many pieces, prose and verse, in *L=A=N= G=U=A=G=E, Talks, O.ARS* and *Boxcar,* in Andrews, Silliman, Hejinian, Bernstein . . . everybody. It isn't fatal, but isn't merely ascribable to a general oatmeal level one may expect; what I want to know is how it may follow from these writers' expectations, as Davie imagined consequences attending the disruption of syntax. It seems to me, in passing, that when (these) (our) moderns do disrupt syntax, as in some of the fictive pieces in *Likely Stories* (Bruce McPherson, ed.) you get warmed-over Gertrude Stein. So my first rule, reading this stuff, is to allow myself to dismiss writing which, thinking it's wonderfully inventive, reinvents (baldly) the playfulisms constructed by Joyce in the *Wake* and Stein in (say) *Geography & Plays, Tender Buttons* of course, and *Geographical History of America.* Let's not, pretending to enlarge discourse, proffer *How to Write* pastiche.

In passing, but having started with Davie, I should mention the amusement it gives me when geniuses who *do* disrupt syntax, or in general ride on a melting edge of disorientation, write phrase after phrase of the sloppy English I associate with white socks and fifties high schools. If your mind is mush ideogramic constructivism won't help.

There *are* techniques which have served almost too long. Imagined contexts. Robert Kelly, in *Likely Stories,* writes a series of ruminations on or from the *root* meanings of Russian words in real (of course unintelligible) texts; it's almost the only Kelly I can read without utter boredom. Tom Mandel has a piece, "from 21 Sonnets" in *O.ARS 3,* retrieving Shakespeare's *Sonnets* from Celan's German. . . .

If purity of diction were German would it ride a horse, the "pleasure of not understanding" not a message but a tooled case in a wallet attached to the saddle with squares of thread with Xes in. We wave to Gadamer on the road.

A symposium on whether charm is important in current writing, or even allowed. My private suspicion, then, is that most writing which announces itself as Jakobsonian if not translative is really ("like they say," Creeley) dried muffins with Symbolist flour.

*Wonderland* prose and De Quincey's aren't syntactically disruptive but can provide, as Davie would say, experiences, etc. We may not be talking about experiences. We'll allow *maybe* that "talking about" is hopeless strategy, and even drab work which thwarts the meaninglust may be *illustrative,* what writing would be about if it could—not "knew how" but had more talent. I don't much like prose or verse handing me by invisible convention, the lucite bucket, experience.

Interpreting a picture is not like interpreting a poem. Interpreting may not be the most exciting part of reading. If it is, we manufacture felicitous finds for each other, like the photographs of trees with wonderful official remarks under that my friend Jim Haining frames, dance contest ribbons, as if the picture above the print were what you thought, or expected to be what you thought.

The big move a long while was, hide the context. This produced Leopold Bloom reverie of the kind Silliman now does easily and adeptly. Allow imaginative frieze and you get phantast dadoes; it doesn't matter if the invasive contexts are private, a shape you can't shake, buckle, thread. Any of these may tease. The boredom of what doesn't allow for my current headache, or never mentions food. This matter of subject: why in so much, is no noun uttered I can't find in *People?* Culture hangs from their throats.

A *pure* speech not ruffled by what a cretin thinks is invention, distressed wood. Food is not interesting *because* it is cooked; the assumption is the American cafe.

Invasive contexts—those sapphires in the mud. Unless you want to say with Wittgenstein that intelligibility is syntactical you don't need that notion for in-little Symbolist conjunctions. It probably makes sense to say metaphors are invasive contexts controlled by grammar. But the habit, as we have it, is more like Sterne as described by Murray Krieger, a healthy sense of disjunct worlds meeting at points or nodes of risibility—and a sense of time as plastic. So, invasive worlds, Uncle Toby borrowing kitchen things to be mortars, and the never expressed pathos of velvety English lawn making do, by reduction, for blood-soaked Flanders or wherever it was. Gulliver at the breast. And that sense of pottering about as what lets worlds meet, metaphor occurring in idleness.

If the motto is words as such no matter how, coupled with the old Symbolist disgust given art, or at the giving of it, and this taken as somehow *like* Gadamerian perplexity at a text, as if everybody were a Swiss passport, no one seems to think the results could be funny. A life report with an inventive top line may be, unless Joyce does it, merely pleasant. Stein in *How to Write* will hit on serious insights considering serial description, a horse and a tree. Two horses. Three. This is a pleasure like Picasso's Homage à Gertrude, a little violence. People come and go in Beckett and Spenser.

Not montage but multiple contexts. Not *Fantasia* as culture. Wittgenstein, looking young and bedeviled, pointing at Russell who is pointing back. Caption: GREAT MOMENTS IN SEMIOTICS #2—Wittgenstein and Russell Ostensively Define Each Other. What troubles me is always what is left out, which can be a vice if you want to save the little things first—cigar crumbs, the frazzle on waistcoat eyehole. A note on guitar dangers in *Rendezvous Newsletter* includes the color sweated into the top of a guitar by an armpit.

What I'm saying is probably that being two places at once should be more fun than it is in recent texts—perhaps from a novelist carry-over, the pretense that non-"present" contexts must be supplied by memory. They should both be lived, like Uncle Toby. What I've come to call Memory Remembered is like those scenes in bad continental horror films, ingenue cellar walks, more Mrs. Beeton than Mrs. Radcliffe. Mummies should be dusty but not cobwebby. Wordsworth remembers a thing, can't get over it, and warms to it as he writes. The not getting over is his living of it.

So, subjects are multiple and the mind skittish. Good philosophers or linguists can make words subjects, or depress even them below the level of subject, as if to forget one's parents, and this may be better than keeping pictures on the desk or mantel. For years Picasso used no model, as a way to be different from Manet, Renoir, Lautrec. We *will* make art out of words, however we can.

And yet, to do this badly. The Language blurbs, poet to poet, are utterly embarrassing in Small Press catalogs. The more fulsome these, the more vapid the booklet. What is reading that we should read. There is a limit how serious we should be about this or, advance entails wit. I should also like it to require a mature urbanity (or rurality), as in Jim Haining's poems nobody caresses. How do you do it in the middle of it, contexts maybe wounding you like arrows, is it for me, writing as a kind of comportment. Do we smile at our sheep. Do they smile back.

# Two Doz. Rom.

Romanticism is a system of habits.

"I have the superstition that human beings have, that when they hear something that matters to them, it's true." Olson, third session, *Poetry and Truth*. This is the sin for this, for that. It's not a recognition. An action in a medium (imagined as a flux, and this includes study): what is significant excites me. This is to say I love my love for how she makes me feel. We ought to be more grown-up about the world than this, allow that the best of it may *not* intrigue, much less be "secrets" the poet may impart.

This desire to do serious work with texts—or glyphs—one *can't read,* is more than flimflam though including a wish to be learned, to impress. Joyce could tell you like a good linguist how much Icelandic he knew—would himself have a notion. Olson's is tarot, vertical motions imagined as horizontal, Le Dantec critiqued.

"Nobody wastes time interpreting what is not thought worth interpretation." Helen Gardner, *The Business of Criticism*.

Arnold's preference for Joubert, and Pound's recommendations (and taste in visual art) may go to or come from one reason. That art is rare, not for everybody, and is sanative, for the ill—sounds like black market.

The pop health writers say you're looking at it wrong, that with a little effort the world will be as you imagine it—or be as if what you imagine it.

Did the Greeks have puppets and if not why not? There should be puppeteers on vases.

Stevenson's idea of romance is, as he confesses, the picturesque *informing* action. One end of it is pastoral.

"The syntax of the description remains distinct from the syntax of the moralizing, and the failure to bring them together is the failure to generate a new syntax, without which there is no poem, and no need of one." Earl Wasserman, *The Subtler Language.*

He after all who elevates mere exuberance into a poetic will write verse like Chesterton's. I think Duncan writes like Chesterton. He talks of the Dark Gods as if they were house cats.

Eighty degrees and the grass overgrown, people in the next house cutting my backyard front—trenches in velvet.

"Acquaintance with a man in the concrete is neither awareness of his bare individuality nor knowledge of the sum of his qualities and activities but a grasp in some measure of the inseparable real unity of his individuality with his qualities and activities." D. J. B. Hawkins, *Being and Becoming.*

"In American politics, minorities lose." Robert von Hallberg, *Charles Olson: the scholar's art.* That one is valuable is not a datum, an achieved result. Park on Hazlitt, what Hazlitt cried up. Carlyle and Coleridge were not the only voices, to Olson's I hunt among stones. It doesn't matter where you quote, is the consequence and we are again medieval. "To write a poetry intended to 'fit audience find, though few' may be a kind of arrogance, but it should be recognized that historical pressures, in the seventeenth century as well as in the twentieth, may demand a choice between what is crudely called elitism and silence."

What tempering does is make the metal bendable rather than brittle; you don't want your ax or sword to break. Why should this need to be said?

It is possible that the Russians resent learning to read, and the packed Vozhneshensky stadia are their nostalgia for a lapsed oral state. Trammell finds this an apotheosis of tribe; it may be healthier that in our country people in obscure towns write. A *Quincy* History. Trammell's Cherokee county. The lone clerk. It is as if, by contrast, Russian writing is never quite silent.

A local hamburger joint sold out to Iranians who changed the name slightly. "Does this ... um ... mean something in Iranian?" Smugly, "Oh, yes." "Um ... what?" *"Cattle Candy."*

Why Lamb Is For Me The Perfect Critic—his letters to Coleridge and Wordsworth about their current verse judge it in terms of tact, almost of decorum; takes them seriously as utterance when their temptation was to claim for verse an ideal area.

Perhaps if there is a simple object in nature a star might be it. In any case, if I happen to look at the heavens and think of unimaginably large gas balls, there is the feeling that it has not helped. Popular science falls between imagine and conceive, and Darwin must become again the perception that there are more dead birds than usual in parking lots.

Louise Glück's *Firstborn,* powerful not overlong poems, passion barely contained, do employ unexpected percepts but not quite as the mind will fix on an irrelevant. I've traced and traced a statuette while talking on the phone, from desperation or a fellow creature-feeling, or sat vacant with one sock on. Hers is Goneril verse, acts of inclusion by a will, as the predator may eat more than it knows. By comparison Maxine Kumin's first book focused more on its sensibility. Thinking of the two makes me wonder if Dickinson is not in a way cruel.

Pull it *out,* passion seeping into the world.

Smearwin wants to go on a trip, and may. A glass oar will do, looked through like Frost's wet pane in "Apple Picking," to see through to what floats (or is moved by the wave's underside, near shore) or is partly visible as Wordsworth said memory almost was. The objection is *to* that caressing of clarity, furniture of glazed refractions, rather than the dumb, muted half-feeling looking at lake bottom objects furred with tan or pea-brown flock coating, the disappointment of shape impermeable, the bottle at best a bottle, even with its fluted cap nonradiant.

How can we hold them in the head without contempt, as for a small thing, enameled countries as in La Vieille Russe, past grandeur in baroque eggs, ivory grooming kits. They did suffer but we did likewise suffer, from last-gasp teachers who thought romance a high thing, straw and hay, yarn and bits of mirror.

This ring, if you put it on, will make you a poet. This poem, if you read it, will make you a poet.

Imagine a drugged puppet.

The flowers need not be made of velvet. Our botanizers were romantics. On tops of buttes or is it mesas I'm told there are tiny flowers. And one sees storms, buttes made of vapor, between them. Deserts teem, and this should have been a romantic remark. Say, of those poets who painted Southwest landscape, their first discovery is carry a lot of white.

# How to Nonread

*What remains when* you write nonreferential art poses the question invidiously, as when people call Gertrude Stein "art by subtraction." I'd rather ask what do the moderns—Bromige, Bernstein, Silliman, Hejinian—do that Stein does not; how much are we invited to a thirties table, objects, food and rooms that are reruns of the fun dinner with Apollinaire and Picasso for Douanier Rousseau. It's easy to dismiss the connection they seem to want to make to John Cage performance pieces, though both propose to alter a medium till it *becomes* an audience's expectations, and "play with that" though without the prop of established conventions. It's better to dismiss all that and appeal to a marginal public, perhaps like the one which collects newspaper headlines (there is a Brooklyn magazine called *Giants Play Well in the Drizzle),* or those (I'm one) given to saying a word out loud while walking, because we've thought of it and we like it.

Defense may be the wrong defense. Yet other writing appears, is good or bad and gets misjudged from how liking gets in the way of principles. Collected editions and reprints respond to tastes more settled. The definition of a "classic" is that it is well distributed. Language-oriented, nonreferential writing appears from Segue, Tuumba, small and smallish presses, and takes its chances on the fringes of the fringes. The presumption is that they like each other, keep up with innovations, and are fond of such horseplay as Charles Bernstein's rewriting Milton lines (in "Entitlement"), retaining nothing but line shape and syntax:

> These tribunes, if any pout, the sentence dormant
> Of florid Calm pesters daily
> Flouncing or with agile succession of mundanity
> Peruse idle in that dented token.

There is a pleasure to seeing this done at all, and it is (I'd say) nothing like jazz transpositions, much less little quotes from other songs introduced as riffs. But this scrap is from quite a long piece, a set of pastoral arias for three "voices," I suppose syntaxes. And of course it isn't intelligible. I've read Bernstein books through, and he's most interesting to me verging on sense, but with a looser notion of relevance, a sort of ultimately gelatine salad of associations, than is taught in College English. *That's* all right; we have traditions of nine-tenths unintelligible poems, from Blake's *Zoas* to *Houseboat Days.* But these writers aren't making French symbolist thickets. The words are more like mouthfuls of Lincoln logs (or crushed clam shells). They don't trip over casements into realms of psychic faery. It can have, even tends to have, no charm, not even the charm of instruction sheets from foreign industrialists.

Language is semisystematic, and leans very hard on expectations. There are some among nonreferentials who define their activity as political, as if meaning is a bourgeois taste—as opposed to the notorious abstractionism of bluecollar labor—or suspect it because transmissibility is too like a transaction. Meaning becomes tainted commodity.

The question for me, as dogged reader who grew up with Christopher Morley pipe-and-slippers training, is whether any of the transformations "reading" undergoes given these texts is accessible to me. More broadly: what sense do these works make shelved in bulk in (say) a rare-book library? Or are we to think of them as tools, carried increasingly scuffed in the pockets of intelligent jeans, as backpackers used to stock Gary Snyder? This may be to think of the printed things as objects when we should be thinking of them as dial readings charting a process. A journal of imaginary physics could claim the same attention, and no more.

Of course I suspect that it's done by people who can't write well in the normal way, and it might be less than invidious to remark that these kinds of writing make it difficult to judge verbal skill. Ultimately their books of verse and stacked paragraphs *may* be taken as remarks about how writing is generated. Bernstein again:

> A fumbling derivation
>
> throttling without deviation
>
> through a tarred pocket with
>
> additional tutelage, up to the
>
> burned decks of a demoted
>
> desquamation.

(Burning Deck is the name of a small press.) Gertrude Stein wrote "A blind agitation is manly and uttermost," and a great many lines like that in *Tender Buttons* and *How to Write.* Ashbery's verse is much more sequential but without context; this is "reserved" as the cookbooks say, and I suppose thrown out. Stein is even too musical, and has the virtues of uttered speech. Her recordings do sound like a Baltimore matron.

Language-poet events are far from these graces, hardly texts (perhaps spray-painted on cement, like gang names on bridge abutments), and "reading" them often means finding a way to make them interesting at all, to recover them from dullness. Bernstein quotes Eigner's remark, "Nothing is too dull."

I am 18th-century trained; Pope is my idea of the first modern poet. He thought dullness the product of dunces. Here it's as if we wade through those awful would-be wits, with our mouths stopped by an "Oh well, we don't intend to be significant in those ways." Interest and interesting are replaced by attention. Lyn Hejinian did a piece lately about all the tables she knew; it skirted the danger of sounding too much like thirties experiment, but perhaps she was ashamed of its thematic unity. A theme piece will engage memory or some kind of persistent retrieval in ways which, as acts, are meaningful.

Swinburne is not a fun poet for me to read (neither is Shelley), because I find them meaningless and pretty, even if they're lisping of horrors. I'm tempted to say, of Shelley, that qualities without quantification are no damn good. The nonreferential poets (if a nonreferential, nonsymbolist poem is a poem) do raise reference as a problem, though their frequent suggestion that any reading for meaning is an automatism is a lie. Still, if one is to read them not own them reasons, even techniques, must be found, perhaps not to defend their texts as much as come up with a reason for their superiority to garment-district catalogues or lists of ingredients.

I have no one sample exhibit (Bernstein's poem about his father comes to mind), but the imagined exemplum I have in mind—it may be significant that an imagined one will do—is wandering through an area of experience known to the poet, which is a kind of limit, but the words and phrases substituting for each other, occurring spontaneously or taken from a text as cue list, are absolutely on a par, themselves experiences. Doing this very well, you'd think, would or should result in Stein or Joyce, but no room is left usually for an almost-caught meaning or consistently liquid, warbling phrase. It is perhaps too many negations, too puritan, saying the meanings I come to will be unexpected, nonsymbolist (not a nonverbal moment "caught"), and a byproduct of words and world considered as hostile systems. The reader is a kind of secret agent of letters, privileged in a way *not* to follow a text.

It isn't much of a fraternity, as the readers of Stevenson or Lamb shared a taste for *this* rendering of experience (or the experiences rendered). I can be a Boswellian but not a Hejinianian or Sillimanite. One is not *grateful* for these texts the same way.

How wisdom creeps in is always a problem, and for these texts any marginal humanity. They are made, and the writers do seem different from each other. I love a writer with expertise, who knows something in a field or can *do* something like train lions. Experience too like other people's beats itself thin, like tapa cloth. Let the words *not* be from a thesaurus, yet unexpected. I *think* the reading is still too much changed to be called reading, but am willing to see the whole activity as as marginally useful as say the scum on hot lead.

# Naked Croquet

Tiny round pearl buttons on shanks, sewn by a hole through to puffed linen near buried in lace, cloth combat, hillocks and piping that should be named like Civil War cornfields, fence and ditch. We photograph women so cumbered against cannibal pots, just what you wouldn't wear, as if people undressed to eat. Or play croquet, foot lately in kid now naked to turf, pressing colonial grass. The joiner has turned these mallets, as Arcadians smoothed crooks with flint knives, woven kirtle, a tool rather than dress. The ribbon a late thing, touch of market color, to be had as they say and quite easy to attach but not *on* the crook till courts make of it a style. Beardsley's dandy, a dude in slippers, is also in Arcadia, with the grace to be distinct from shrub, no quick rustle of cloth and into the bush, satyr with current hair. Cloth and starch protect you at all points. The maid likewise would *be* a maid, found naked, her puff cap with telltale black ribbon adjacent, wrapped in cloth like a cheese. Buttons would not look out of place on a Stilton or Wensleydale. It is as if there are *no* ways to pass from (say) *Alice* to a teeshirted youngun. Hence the Pennyroyal Press attempt is magnificent *as* going beyond period, for not concentrating on cloth. Tenniel's pictures of Gladstone and Disraeli are always most beautiful (after the eye orbits) around the toes of shoes. It makes one fetishist. A Victorian gentleman in wool (to preserve it) underwear in a Danish bog would have so many parts it would be like rats' teeth in desert sand, no way to tell from the staining if his top hat started white. Designs in his pocket. Besides *Alice* we got detective novels, which are read with tea and the clothes (Reginald Fortune noting what flowers are up under the body) are clues but a custom. Murdered people are clad. The Ripper, getting at his women, is in a way ultimately undressing them. Toy theater Whitechapel sets would have tabbed skirts and shawls. We then have toy placards, signs to advertise the play, *outside* in a toy street, passersby and paned shopwindows like a Bond Street can, Thackeray indolent in a corner, sketching. Tell me this is out of period. A surprising range of interesting books first appeared in 1888.

# Scale and Interest

*If* interest is liking or like liking scale wouldn't matter, miniature Eiffel Tower (Williams's paperweight pyramid he imagines as a golf tee), Lincoln Memorial, Albert Hall across from him seated inside—not guarded by—elephants and camels. Spring clothespin buildings impinge, classy as oreo edging, and the guard stopped us picking pennies out of the dried wading pool by Rodins not interesting except the torso, those by others even less. Returned ones rolled under the homage to Debussy Pan with alpensyrinx and goats, one at D-Art horned skull and plated pipes. My photograph of Liberty's hand and torch sticking up out of a booth with "literature" has visible on the railing just below the flame two people.

On a roof slope like a cut emerald the four or five inches of wrist are installed slant. The forefinger's first two joints are one's height. Behind pagodas, kiosks, tent like a lampshade and STATUE OF LIBERTY on a board just readable above a drawing or painting of the projected island. Description is interminable. And we are told, having got brochures in the mail, its iron rots. The torch is *like* a turned thing, base of a hurricane lamp with bent-out points to receive the shade, or any of them held at stair bases by Indians.

A very large beer can held down by guy wires inflated beside a building was visible a while (you see them places) near the restaurant on a rise with the waterfall ad. The sense of tension in a moderately large thing, or the feeling of continuous creation. A very large crystal ball for instance would be quite different, and this affects science-fiction mockups of domed cities. How much detail before the underside of a starship gains satellite mass. It was a mistake to make the Nautilus look like a fish. A vision of clouds (moving slowly) seen through eyeholes in a statue gives that sense of shift, the outside inside. Noldes at the Primitive show were about the size you expect, *Demoiselles* and the head of Marie-Thérèse much larger than art books suggest, hers like a very large shrub, part of the effect, picture a wonder in Dallas with blue lines (feathered out at the front foot) for final definition, which he'll not do again though Cézanne still could.

I did two drawings (before a guard stopped me) of Gaudier-Brzeska's "Head" of Ezra Pound at the Dallas Museum, the head at the top a model for the "Hieratic Head" in marble, and as I went down the figure in two tries never hit bottom—the sculptor seemed to get too interested in local curves, angles, outcrops, in his invention as a European competing with adzed fetish. At least it raises where in a tall thin thing one is, and I count it significant that though I can always draw a whole thing my failures here are this sculpture and the Scott Memorial in Edinburgh.

That there might some day be no more cakes and ale, burning bannocks on a hot stone. Local sculpted rower with knees, arms, bit of boat coming out of the floor separately like atolls off Australia. Principle of the cyclorama, easier not to focus on where you know it is. One is not imagining a giant Liberty under the earth.

A crystal held by a god in a bush (Moses and Gideon) seems almost clear, no little Heidelberg town in it, down by the palm, Gideon's helmet a streamlined pot, nearly finned. The orb under the helmet would refract light from the eye slit. In theory all the action around is in it. That's the effect of it in the picture. Schwitters's "For Kate" is mostly about cartoon elbows and fists disposed or blanked by tissue over, heads in a loose circle around the central figure except one King George on a bit of envelope canceled (by a Greenwich hand stamp) looking out.

Why is it easier to see a doll's house as haunted than an oversize palace (even with sealed rooms)? The little printed book on the shelf is more likely wicked than a folio. Bachelard studies the nutshell house but not as malign. Again metaphors (from light physics) of concentration, focus, or the inertial point through which a vertical line drops, Poe's gold-bug, oversetting sailboat, Rodin's figure's line mostly through space (even Matisse's dancer's foot has it). Pisan Reflections, the line rather than a shaded column such an abstraction. The Louvre's caryatids never had arms; these sheared planes show them in *section.*

Say, the Sephiroth with physiological, astrological and tarot grids laid on them can have no dimension in a different way from an architect's rendering with no scale for the trees, the glossy perspective and exposed-fin beams. Analogies are not spatial.

Andre's face in the film is very large, really quite large, and this is as if one is close to it, as one can see all Patton's tanks in the background, far distance, but small, lines on the actor's face, eyes engaging yet mocking, occasional self-forgetful intensity. Grotowski's forest as arena then to dine out on, ending in narration, burial as narration *while* being very large. The size is an inadvertence like the tailor's stitches, to allow a style to emerge. This pen's blue ink comes out unfluidly, not "grudgingly"—the pen does not hoard. Yet it tries the mind trying to think on. Left to ourselves we admire the soft collar, the food. A potato could have been shown in like closeup to like effect. A British coin, like my cufflinks with the traitor's gate on the back, and I've seen that design on a forehead.

As the eye with eyebrow and lazy descenders inscribed verso Dr. Who makes a talisman in yellow. There's a cursive form (arguably anything not two colors is cursive.) Gaudier's birds.

Gauguin's self-portrait in the McNay, on quite rough canvas (only not the sacking he did good Polynesians in) has an idol to the right like a ginger jar, but is his black and red striped tie and eyesocket to nose planes as if cosmeticized—and gains in reduction as if more drybrush than the original actually is. Some Cézanne apples and oranges are thinner close to and actually please less (one has imagined the folded tablecloth as thick.)

Animal cracker lions on a round cookie tin. The red and yellow (gold) designs are meant to bring the wagons to mind.

Neiman alien cookies, on doll bodies by a girdered spaceship in a small display window by the chocolates.

Scale is in a way generic, as if one could strike an average size. Crow's building with the Rodins occurs within parameters. Bob says the Primitivism show gets bad reviews in national magazines. It is neither too large nor too small. But referring to things in it installs "the" everywhere, objects as representative.

The last place I saw Charles Olson underrated was a reprint of Dickey's crystal-gazing piece making fun of the programmatics. I would say that anyone who titles a poem "Issue/Mood" is *automatically* to be taken seriously. The Vancouver Language-poet conference is this weekend, and he might not even be mentioned. You could ask what happened to the full-tilt poem, in which you covered yourself with pinned messages, feathers, spools, things like forks balanced there, and then moved forward with it falling off you. It is journalism to take it farther, but that was a good way to write, doing justice to what situation was there, what the poem in a way knew was relevant—not *just* an uprush of presorted things, but as if a consciousness were being built on the page (a quarter-inch above it).

There is such a thing as a "downy flake" (in Frost). This is a remark about poetic diction.

The intelligence that gnomes have, Skeat says Clio found. They know where things are buried.

I had painted a little *Faust in His Study* which I think David Searcy now has, and put colors on a cheap frame to bring it closer to the picture. David, told this, said you'll have to frame the frame. This was more a surprise to me than Whistler's "Why not frame the sonnet?" said to Rossetti. In my pocket's a cast brass fake Roman coin I need polished but not plated.

Reading Turnbull's *Thomas Wolfe,* and full of books on Coleridge and Hopkins to read and half-read, a Shelley pair and Murry's *Keats and Shakespeare* to supplement Ricks, I come back to the Old Critics— Mackail included and I wish I had Bradley's lectures on Wordsworth again—to be among people who were stirred (the woman who wrote about *memorizing* Tennyson as a child), and how is it that among fits the one group, as if the physicality of authorship were more its.

A gray toy. It may be significant that the bodies of machine-transforming warriors (those parts which in a way survive or persist through transformation) are gray. The matrix may be gray, seven swords through her heart or not. Or—a gray is only not a white (for exteriors); something of inner limb inheres in gray.

You've got to understand, watching her leaf through a notebook (glue in psychological scraps) how important the stillness of writing down notes on cases must have been for the pioneer psychologists. What curves these hooks bring back, making compression conventional. We found small trilobite-like armored things in the dry leaves after the big storm, last days of September, and find they're firefly larvae hatched this spring—blunt as a trebled earwig, that kind of presence. Down 200 in the big field by the tall white house, lights so bright we wondered could they even be fireflies. Maybe it aids dispersion. Had I installed it *at the time* in a notebook the models would overpower, page a witness as well as memory, tarring to residue. Mice in a teaspoon or a saddlemate of Roy Rogers's nostalgic tent show, dreamed.

Storrs with its longhilled model farm does not, at all, look like Ark cutouts. And giant cows seen on a back road in Putnam looked diluvian but again not much like black and white dappled ones in plywood. Cows do remind you of cows, do not imitate art. Pigs surpass their drawings by greater grace of line. Cows transcend by bulk.

The black and red striped tie on Gauguin might be a dickey, the puff of spotted white a bow—or is that a handkerchief?

Van Gogh's "Railroad Bridge," seen in a house raised, moved and turned into each other from three separate buildings, is a four-dimensional box. Color can call to color in ways that mimic the dimensionality of luminosity (the echoing halls of Hegel's thought). The square columns in pictures of salt mines are these leftnesses, as if the reverse of a building could be made in marble. I think there's no analogue for it in a picture, not even the negative. Yet the question of Gauguin's tie is a bit like it.

This is not interesting, as if scale is invulnerable to paragraphed examples, Francis Bacon feeling gold, deciding heat is motion. No discipline for adepts, jigs to turn Elsie Stevens's face (a clay slab) into Liberty tiny, the letters *cut* with patently Roman care, not serifed from standing up, pillboxes and dykes.

In Michigan I saw the other Gauguin, Delacroix they say instead of idol upper right, and the same ambiguity (handkerchief) around the chin-stroking hand that to me enforces a notion that both proceed from one sketch, since the color's different but placement equivalent and you've his repeating horse compositions as if panels in larger paintings to show he did it elsewhere, the brutality of proof, canvas equally nubbly to the mind annihilating time (this immediacy of being *in front* of a picture). Carpeaux's "Spirit of the Dance" took me back to the Petit Palais, his "Smoker" to Fort Worth's fiddler that my ballpoint brings back too, the oddity of master copies of Rubens or Delacroix replaced by postcards.

The scale goes first in a tiny copy, raising contrasts to Daumier. His "Le Peintre" I took away in ballpoint in front of my Smithsonian datebook, so tall even with space around I had to do the top twice to get a curve on the light behind the hat. These edges in him are, of course, the picture, and as finely tuned (what he *is* after) make copies of him hard to do; a leeway's gone.

Blocking a thing—sizing the main bit, tree, nude curve—tells your sheet what the margins will come to. So midpanel strokes matter right to the edges, four by convenience and you chop off a bit to get equivalent shapes, or float all (daring a temptation to play to the paper's edge, very like "rhetorical stress" creeping into scansion).

"The illusion of wordless thought is central to the classic mind-body dualism. . . . The *Cogito* hence must be silent." Fraser Cowley, *A Critique of British Empiricism.* Standing with the Late Monet book and *thinking* of the Houston Museum "Japanese Bridge," which I went over with a magnifying glass, is like that. We're told the bridge in place is startlingly small, and so (the travelers add) in the pictures it's *nearer* than you imagine.

It may be (reading Martin's introduction to *Eliot in Perspective)* that a sense of scale is like the perception of allusion. Not that I understand Hollander's Greek in *The Figure of Echo,* or what an audience for allusion would be. But modern allusions, for instance, are neither public nor private, and this not always in verse which hasn't decided if it's heard or read (is that a difference, for allusion, incidentally?) Dickens begins a gothic tale and one recognizes and welcomes narrative, being told a story, then a traditional invasion of the ordinary by ghosts, special knowledge, corpses, dead frogs . . . one is in the palm, reduced to "The Kind of Act of," reading glasses now off.

Why was that not adequate as thinking is a pretty question. There is an imagining of *results,* perhaps a schoolboyish marveling at a sum that can be checked. Again the primitive notion of chemistry *experiment* as a hazard. The animal may be a target. The metaphors fail—a process, like the vinegarmakers paying Pasteur. Austin says "like" can save the pig because a different (Aquinas would say analogous) order from a species-designation; to see consequences *of* this is the second-best "kind" of thinking, the best Wittgenstein or Heidegger bored with two self-proving assertions facing each other. Query if a touch of this excitement is in Kant's decision to talk about antinomies, as if he could give a recipe for transcending them. It's as if he saw the pairs as like (I was saying) listening to a highschool student just discovering "If God can see everything then why," etc. The soul is numbed, bored by this overhearing; Kant kept awake by saying oh well, these go in pairs.

Boots made of a substance might have a star pressed in outside, and this stained a different color from the boot, both polished to one finish. The star's boundary will be a color difference *and* a texture perhaps less visible xeroxed, as some contour maps pretend to pitted raising or seas in weals. So the map color-problem could be done with textures, the boundaries traced (a velvety *patch).* If a candle is made of a real stub top and bottom rolled in cartridge paper, pinching the middle is experience to the Edwardian conjurer. Herrmann may have had a little black sack kept open with whalebone between his knees at parties. The boot made of metal is like a toy train.

Hamlet's mother mother mother mother mother is, in cursive script, written without raising the pen. The repetition enforces connection. For what word would this not be so?

"There is an essential poignancy and idiocy in emotion itself." Danby, *The Simple Wordsworth.* I've seen ads today for rag-content Record books and coveted a nine dollar one, and have had a kind of feeling for ones called "bound journals" in them, thinking of Boswell. To start any book in a bound form grasps the intent to make a book, pages thin to transparency no bar, like any sheaf of handwritten onionskin looked at from the back. It's already gone, as fairy money supposedly becomes old leaves or (oddly) the flick to the frame's placard first. Those gilt tablets at any rate give off an odd light. As little cakes as said give off an odd conceptual aura, the pits that develop in pancake tops ink dots in children's books.

What constitutes a largish portion, as of Chicken Almond Ding, a disconcerting serving, is as usual its relation to one's body. It should be all right in a company, but even a twenty-pound turkey is a portion, anything that fits a plate. A platter is the largest plate that is not a tray. Yet I don't think this is greed; table fellows are desired. The problem of Other Minds is discussed at Cambridge over lunch, and at Oxford over lunch. Trinity (Dublin), by Hegelians.

And so to dismissal, my lecture on the cognitive import of losing a taste for ... the soul as sustaining and perceiving Ego-bearer (and, unthinkably, the problem of immortality) ... perception itself, as only halfway real, "sense data," and then ethics, morals, what you'd think as founded in experience would still pay off a little (I can still wear an Inverness), top hats for Harvard overseers like a boys' school grown old, the nominalist debate however described. These *were* and now *aren't,* as a Victorian person might lose a sister or two. We can't simply say the posing of the problem alters. Here is Kenny's *Descartes* and Curley's *Descartes Against the Sceptics*— wonderful leafed through. The sign, academically speaking, a problem's being dropped is that a philosopher's answers to objections are used to infer what he once meant. Coleridge's earnestnesses in the *Biographia* may be plotted yet again, yet one feels in spite of his thinking the whole man thinks (whole poet philosophizes) a gap between his core and these problems, not just these statements of these problems. Gods die as concerns die, maybe only the political left. Subjects one thinks will automatically get a hearing, board on which the one thing needful is placed as a counter.

How many poor clerics have sat and said *ex animum* or something, thumbing a leaf, repeating a phrase just read or an invasion, for the comfort of being there being invaded like solemnity at a public event. The word or words or language carries with it enough of this concern, ambient import. It's not there in a nosegay even remembering flowers have meanings. It is more like ascribing to the particular flower remembering. Abilities may be referred to things, how much can the spoon hold. Why doesn't the mark from a nonlitho blue pencil on the *back* of an onionskin page copy?

The Gauguin looks at you assessing rather than speculatively, eye whites a green-blue (Bacon's Van Gogh Self-Portrait head or rendering of Blake not a fist or knee of flesh with a mouth looks at you or might look.) The whole problem of a virtual real distance. The cover painting for the expensive Sargent book, woman with a lavender bow is met in Edinburgh, kittycorner from Daumier's "Le Peintre" oddly large for him but still backlit head, bust, tall for its width. She is wider because in a chair. We are wider because dressed warmly with matching Scotch House scarves like fieldmice though it's May, and a Monet haystack is cool as if snowy. We approve Louveciennes. Europe is a face if it is an identity that is an aspect, brushes in a pot can be faces from the lightslick long on them, and the number for brush width alters if there's a smear of paint farther down the shank, as if a better identifier. Constable's "On the Stour" is the best little picture in the world.

# The Prose Object

Provincialism is not necessary but desirable, as to get something out of Swinburne's Study of Shakespeare. I'm thinking of the people who call Poe provincial. The other is a fear of being known, seen around, made of glass.

The wasp-waist silver-nickel cup holder with paper cone full of cold water fades into Picasso's painted sculpture, the glass with painted polka dots a surprise.

Life without sympathy—today I opened a spongy avocado and found the nut almost free of the shrunken, discolored but not spoiled pulp, the shock again as of cobwebs around seamed faces. If one sewed the avocado shut. One wonders if Pater's "curiosity" constitutes an impatience with the normal. What we have allowed, the mock cut-glass of the saltshaker, crackle black spring napkin dispenser, moves slowly away leaving the plants which stamped the shaker tops (and plated them?) discarded or buried whole, approximating to the meaning of archeology.

A licked stamp, for instance, pressed down then brushed across with the finger may move, slide to a second posture, leaving a record of this in glue on the envelope. The jump is felt as unpleasant because we are never sure the glue will stick in the new place.

"Mourning Becomes Electra." "Tea at the Palaz of Hoon." Their titles were themselves. Pater and Valéry on Leonardo were enough to give Stevens Wordsworth as Hoon, though the mock-philosophical approach is like Coleridge—whose titles (*Sibylline Leaves)* were awful. Contemporaries wear cheap gold rings stamped *Karatclad* 18 KT H.G.E. with a large rectangular emerald. Coursey having glued it in added his tc. I found it in the dump of "A Thing About Language for Bernstein" and it's large enough to wear over dress gray gloves, black suit and raincoat, derby for the parade with tiny, tiny transparent stein with green beer in.

But is provincialism the opposite of exclusions, the adequate weight of a shell casing ashtray, an object allowed, prior to decoration. Fred Allen did not juggle on the radio. Perhaps the objects we have when small are real, a pressed-steel black telephone with metal dial that we once painted white so badly, or large cardboard cartons stuck with gas station trash bulbs to be machines.

Cloth in heaps occurs in heaps, depressing in cardboard cartons in garages. One wants to eat out, or burst free of possessions, the stored. Every object is the result of parameters within which it does not crystallize or combust. Imagine the yellow-green of an early cathode tube, recording something.

Six round balls in a tart pan were cork cadmium coated then a mandarin red rolled in the palms, inch and a quarter five clustering around a center, vivid against aluminum but not like fruit. They are drying or I think of dust filtering on them slowly. Three brass cups mouth downward with rings brazed to the bottom will each hold a ball.

That objects have needs is probable; a poorly cared for collection. I've seen designs abashed. If a theater makes models vulnerable, it invites an action. Close to sentimentality, consider the waterfront set for *Dead End,* pilings for the orchestra's East River, the audience with slum notions. Toy theaters are theatrical; circus miniatures aren't. The stage as a place to contain light begins to contain or work with it. No one does a burned theater, a wrecked circus train. Our galactic films make texture a kind of shadow.

The bilge of ships moves sluggishly like bilge or stomach contents.

People who show you money in the hand and then alter it. Two copper coins, silver. We drop hands full of red thimbles into the derby. If grease paint is heavy enough perspiration can dislodge it from (say) the tip of an eyebrow.

Engraved seals and so on exist as if on a par with other objects, produced the same way. So references to carving now in verse really mean moulding. Car names are written in chrome on cars. Duplicating that effect in titles is now standard, and looks better than mock neon.

There is a very good argument that Eleusis was augmented by hallucinogens. Why do I not believe it? that is not how we think of the ancients as having used drugs. It is too much the stage set, bad engravings of hollow statues with priests behind. One does not place a trained snake under the altar, not and get it engraved on semiprecious gems.

I have just put a little calibrated thermometer in the trash. What will it measure underground?

That tin cans are cylindrical accommodates a seam. I've painted one red for tea, and drawn another with spring and banker clips, paintbox, and when I said a mountain of chairs to my father as a drawing exercise he said crumpled kleenex.

Closing the gate in the dark my foot touched and rolled or moved an extended body, soft against the dry dirt. I used to be bothered by walking through single-strand webs, then thought of us both as inhabitants and for a while had no trouble. In *Snow White* the cottage includes insects, and in this respect is peasant art.

Inclination follows habit. If you live solitary objects matter. In offices they are probably like animals. Rolodex. Milking stool. There are office pastorals. The agent in Len Deighton links paperclips, and this is observation as proof the fiction is real. I was almost concerned whether a pinking shears might edge news clippings better. Folds in forties papers hold up. I found out what happened to Vincent Coll in the phone booth, spattered with panes of sugar glass.

Clay imitates reed baskets (which I don't know how to make). But Lunsford's Peruvian pots want to imitate animal skins inflated, the extreme periphery of the animal. It's too easy to say a handle tail or mouth spout is a pun; the weaving skill existing now as obscure projections, so was this to hang it or hold down the lid, does justify Olson's living on the ground, as does a study of color. Are the Peruvian uplands clear, limpidly liquid, misty? The Appalachian woman looks out her kitchen window and sees flowers. The need to have a pot look like an animal which may be edible, feeds into a rake or broom made of broom. We made lifesize dummies of stuffed clothes and rubber masks in our dark basement. It's hard to get a waist's flat width, stuffing.

Since there was no heat generated except a tiny spark behind red plastic, the disk vanes on a Buck Rogers blaster did not dissipate barrel heat, were an intolerable weight and impediment to holstering. That a weapon so destructive should be clumsy in use may be a carryover from the war, uniforms like textbooks, drab, and hardware which looked very good but was always heavy in miniature. Tents likewise taxed strength, and resisted mildew by smelling worse. It was probably Victorian solidity done in metal. There is a fellow here who knows where all the dumps are, pitted square bottles, corks. Very well. But the hospital dump had thin glass, like car fuses with metal ends.

Provinciality, the being in a province, will depend on playing with things, whipstock sockets or other, including clumsinesses like trying to hammer with a screwdriver handle.

The pea green of monel metal.

Larkin's Pantheon, a crude thing of canvas and socketed rods, not good in any wind, has photos and souvenir exhibits of what it's like to have a taste only for local products, as if "having a taste" in any other sense were economically contemptible. Yet to approach objects in this way at all is to have left union neighbors.

Electrical wiring and hurricane fences are about equally mysterious, and I have had lectures on cams and history of pipe. We are also looking for a book on pull toys. The Empire children's pencil (anchord lead) draws well and the vinyl case of my cheap magnifying glass says Hong Kong. Everything is made somewhere.

They are around us, *wrapped* in them or set in them as a box of toys, dairy carts (never with ice), slats for brown logs, there as illustrators find mannikins, thrown bears, a picture. Wristwatch straps or knobs off pots aren't meant to be unattended, or have a limit in use. Sentiment creeps into model train tracks not used paint cans, as a "fluid" the ether. The velvet case for the Lee commemorative pistol includes triangular sections with brass knobs at opposite corners. We will have bullets and no. 11 caps but no cleaning rods.

Everything can be faulty in heat. Beings rip wings off airplanes. U-shaped jaw arcs extend, become angles under stress. The moon has not been sensitive to me a month, left or deserted. Little cased wood whuffles, trilobite cousins, race through my mulch.

Rinsing tea with milk out of the bottom of my cup with tea evokes not the Mass ritual abstractly but the water in gentle larrups, sometimes the odor. Ex-altarboys raise a cup to indicate enough.

Lives in bowls, the fish moving, fish events, captive, hermit crabs in glass shells. Animals should have zippers like missals with fold-down edges.

A young puppy in the yard played with by Mayan children nearly becomes an object. They call to it, Milton or something.

Coleridge's "sumject" and "omject," fronting or trying to front the world in spite of his gaudy diction is like making pottery, the hope that the colors will deepen and not wash off. To have a handle on it (rolled thin, vermiform, so easy it would seem to pull off) or a pedestaled foot, perhaps to isolate heat (for effect, or imagined stability). Coleridge, then, looking at the tea in the bottom of this cup, thinking of brandy or a chop while the Wordsworths eat buttered toast. Is the tea reassurance, or the tint against cup bottom a deceit.

The transparency of mason jars is not evident, peaches or cherries in syrup, the fruit-shaped container with silver leaf lid (with stem and spoon) stocked by the grocery above the registers, fresh ones visible in bins. We have processed them into themselves.

The past won't let itself be reexperienced. That is why possessions are peculiar. One could manufacture false objects dependent on bizarre power sources. A habit as of going unshod might take a while to reconstruct. The Dogon are Victorian. Masks are objects in the present. So, as found in the dirt, are buckles that used to be harness.

In time of trouble draw a human torso and incorporate a text behind which breasts flower or secrete, groin of leaves. This text, about how apples are real, is framed in wood sections in the shape of an apple. It should take hours to stipple the leaves, draw the tiny seedlike cells there being texture or skin depending. Deliberate labor makes a thing.

The prickly feel against the ridge just below the phalanges of a circular openwork faucet handle, will go with black rubber hoses gradually cracking with cotton inside linings, and the water coming out of these is different, *is* different, more iron scrapped in the garbage bogs. Rubber dolls and balls crumble in gardens, applied paint (on eyes) defining the thinnest integument.

Some animals like armadillos translate to materials well. Meandering twigs make snake wands for the Texas Kid. This is not quite like Eskimo sculpture, fat curves as fur, the dream of animal as oleo.

This morning in the Militaria window: a cutaway house with soldiers, I suppose German, running on the ground floor on loose planks, smoked wallpaper and picture, a tank right through the house side. (Upstairs a fallen machine gunner and two tiny upright cases.) The outside a litter of bricks and a street lamp without its lamp. The powdery gray and dun of the models, in the light through the window, made it perverse theater.

On the Greater Dallas phone book, April '83—a telephone lineman nearly up a shattered pole, wire cutter in hand (all this in neatly tinted bronze; he could be a fisherman, cowhand) with, you see, real cable to cut, for him to cut, as tiny dishes are for dolls to eat with. Better that than a telephone puppet, though in its way a puppet for management. It rests on a turned-wood base.

In a shoe shop with a plastic rhododendron up from a brown fluted papier mache pot, two or three leaves per center section. The leaves snap on to moulded sockets like electrical jacks. Shelves seven shoe-boxes wide and three high. Above the mirror a farm boy with bridled pole waving to old man, horse, child, across a wood bridge by a mill, neat highshouldered living house in the pearl-rose distance.

Today's object was a book—the Bruce Rogers *Compleat Angler,* short squat Aldine shape, good paper and a short-across text, fish dimly visible through the unslitted leaves, ghost fish, as in Perkins chapel we were then told that Margaret's death is a kind of error.

Dark things, stone things. Poe liked to think he thought of them, though there are few sculpted figures and no wings—nothing like a marble lobster coming out of the medium, however pitted or cracked. He doesn't like to *touch* rigid materials. A toy locomotive should be heavy, cast. Otherwise everything is really cloth, bronze mummy falling forward, folds in a Balzac, horses with wire armatures barely holding the wax together, a world falling apart from a will to flexibility.

Bricks abut. Gears engage. All buried things share in augmented density. I want to be thinking about anything in lucite, roses in cubes on end (the corners flattened for more reflections), coins, watch parts. Trapped or on perpetual display, celastic raincoat, fleshcolored stocking objects imitating phalli, the sacred joke. Al Flosso liked a beer bottle you squeezed from which emerged an embarrassingly colored member.

I can't but think that what Beaker folk carried with them, how they conciliated coastal Barrow farmers and herders, was distilled alcohol. Though they had metal they did not lean hard on it, and those curved-lip cups would be good theater and pleasant for drinking millet whisky, grape brandy. It's just the technique to precede, as trade, a metal economy. They will have worn caps.

Bury Henry Ford? Dig a large deep pit and line the walls with planks. Pour in a bit of lucite. Build a steel latticework box—floor and sides on the lucite and pour another foot. The body in a car wrapped in plastic is lowered in. The open metal top is bolted on. More lucite to cover. The steel beams are for strength.

Do not be known for any of it. The Danubian adze might have been a miner's tool, device to get metal. Everything except display cases ends up displayed. In New York the harbor and island of Bora Bora, water a lighter green under glass sea, better than boxwood wave over initial C. Things unwrapped from camels would include treasures, like my kitchen shears.

It is so sad, with the passage of years—not the passage of years— that we do what we did, collaborating with Europe till it went with the tin hats, Olson's "Quantitative Verse" as if to show he could write something *like* Eliot's *Selected Essays.* Rubber bars to be forced by the gorilla a cliché like the shotgun Y, cartoon effects happening to involve matter, as pebble tools *are* their dotted pictures, so like stone, charming in line cut, or Whistler's doodles on a survey plate. A site is a rallying point.

Now they recede, into the higher limpidity, De Quincey in his cottage framing visions, study of milk jugs and hearths, a fly (lovely word) against bottle glass—we know how to build below the wind, take advice of locals. Books are imports. Years later the drearier Anglican books, by country pastors and determined, perhaps maritally unhappy city ones, go on boats to Dallas, Jesus' stock. Hard to find a 1611 King James. I demildewed the Bible collection in Ireland, black fine-line morocco retaining dusty lunar discolorations against a soft rag, having earlier cataloged disestablishment pamphlets (and how to feed the family, on jowl). Something of the smell stays in bookshops on the quays.

What he did, the man who came in from New York, was paint a jar of flowers talking into a microphone about how he did it, the people came out and one large woman carrying (taped in a heavy frame) the picture. I passed a note saying ask has he seen the Manet show and he had. I asked it partly because his pictures were so dark. *Flashed* a smile, *flashed* eyes, saying catalog prices, but the manner, neurasthenic recognition, designed to reassure and overpower, made me wonder, as if he lives under a hill being a bad lag-impressionist, the highlights last. I gave away two inks of him working.

"So much talk they had to get through," this of H. G. Wells, and did he meet Jack the Ripper in 1888, the medical training similar. History as idlest conjecture, put forth as up to date, will in later years talk about frogs on a roof playing musical instruments, illuminated from below. They turn in short arcs as they play.

A bad drawing of someone, framed 8x10 in a bar, the darkness of line of lip, incised eyelashes Egyptian around pupils, nose a lump with nostril flare, lump, downward line for cheek, and a matching at mouth corner to show that flesh is a slab, oh wrong these delicate layers, across the street a cat newly dead, few ants just beginning to crawl around the shut mouth.

Here is an object, two-color Everson "holiday greeting" from Oyez:

> Here from the valley floor the long rock sleeps
>  in the sky;
> Length over length the steep walls gather and lift till
>  the far top dims,

and what is wrong with this is object-word and ongoing present-tense verb. Does the object do this at night? No thought for cosmic rays. It is as the observer wills. Objects persist. Even paper, the man's fantasy of his Bible crumbling into little missiles. Bit of pumice, foam rock, not much good in David's sling. Goliath reads Stevenson and depends on his bronze sword with the iron core. We bind our handles up with tar or blood—those knife handles that are stacked leather rings—and anything wrapped around a blade is this war magic comfort.

The difficulty is felt as one's own stupidity or thickness. For us to move among, I like it that bricks have names, and the iron disks in pavement, asphalt, a thoughtful brown with if the city is large enough its name.

I'm just old enough to remember milk wagons cooled with block ice. Stopped, you could watch water drip over the figured iron step, with monumental deliberation, and my parents' current house still has a milk chute. Little reddish brown points, government pressed-paper tokens, and the pillowlike rectangle of margarine with embedded sullen red capsule you broke with thumbs and kneaded with hand warmth, till all came yellow. Coursey made his boy a pull wyvern, stylized thick wood and chromed bolt ends, wings hunch-flap and gryphon head up and down, toy become block, and I was thinking of how tiny bottles might be carved but what would you do for the block ice, fallen chunks with the larger greenness in them, and where did they ride on the truck? It is like bread and butter sandwiches, the slices made of wood, or the fried eggs I saw today, quite small, that stuck to metal shelf uprights.

Spoerri did a topographical map of his worktable and issued a catalog, like Victoria's, of descriptions—the tiny pocketable items which since Stein and Picasso are *trendlich*. Enormous queen (but short) to be in silver-gilt on her own table, with the compotes with dogs and dead rats. What went wrong, this particularity of mixed materials, as Georgian verse didn't number the cattails or the river. There are marsh imaginings; what is a silver thistle letter opener? In the street everywhere with disposable beverage closers are red plastic moulded tail lights, each different, and lately a brass key for a lock like my new bicycle's that didn't fit, bars of an electric heater seen in a trash barrel Monday, after a visit to the gallery with African masks, royal carved throne-stools, crescent wood boxes and carved bowls—perspiration dried on everything. No seeds caught in a headdress, images of the wearer (except beautifully stylized)—take us, little red plastic brakelight, you have been rendered by Mahaffey as (in the middle) a whitehot yellow, but that was in Manhattan.

The horse runs away with the ship. Model horses don't run, because they need a space (like a toy theater) to run in. Similarly clouds even in currently fashionable mobiles don't float, aren't *in* the air they're in. Tilstrom bows at the end, his hands animals. I have seen toasters with card-stock lithographed toast popped up. A small dragon or dinosaur projects a mythic space—as if one could make a puppet of a puppet though this never seems to work. Inside Joseph Cornell's boxes is metaphysics.

The family as illiterate, not a place of learning, satisfied us a long time. So there were cakes for feast days, ornaments from discardable plants, not much light, square bins for running water, artificial pools, as later one would sink a worn-out bucket. Is there no word like hearth for trapped water. And the razors as if set with microliths, turn the bronze fish or bird and water comes out of the phallic tap.

You take the flat wood trap with the rat on the cover and screw in a large screw eye under the staple holding the restraining arm. This satisfies the need to alter. I slide a crust of bread under the bait notch and wrap ten inches of white thread around that. The trap flips over on the animal, and may move a minute or two after. Its tail is longer than live inspection recalls.

I have a little bridey flat in foil to eat and what good are foods shaped like instruments or including baked-in symbols. Hanson mailed a municipal building design, dome and flung windows, over the door rendered as if chiseled APPROPRIATE INSCRIPTION.

It is not the fact that Leibniz could not allow two identical apples, but that he could not allow apples which are mirror images. I said to myself upsetting the board is not part of the rules of chess, and seemed to recall it happens in *Pogo,* raising the question of how a game of chess may be *in* a comic strip. The animals do not make announced moves, but even if they do it is "chess"; a represented game is no game, the philosopher's apple, even if an apple, no apple. Two mirror-image philosophers might resolve this if they could talk. A single issue of a journal, and its plates. We're back to Tenniel drawing backwards on boxwood, though by then it's a plate. These framed never satisfy. One feels one has a hyper-original and this is a trick. Dreyer, having photographed a chess game in black and white, projects the negative. Ladies are asked to remove their hats. The magician, in black, borrows a black hat. Those lightcolored animals (much less birdcages) are a remark about emulsion. If round fruit is produced back then it is oranges, which are exotics. Limes would do, you'd say, as their reverse, but George Jean Nathan objects to green on stage and fruits are costume. Gainsborough made little tray gardens, mirror lakes, pebble boulders, and Tiepolo's models were wax. This is scale, which may have to do with the irreversibility of time. The old magician, finding fruit under the cups, is pleased by the cloth under.

It is good practice to disassemble paper matches, take the staple out and separate the cardboards, peel off the striking surface, glue photographed books or something to the outside of the wrapper and reattach the striking surface, fold the matches in and staple.

It is not a solution, the big paintings of ketchup leavings translucent in the bottle—even tiny models under lucite of littered subway entrances, though on a table with no apparent space for the stairs to go this would be interesting. David, our authority, says the rock wall behind the cave painting must never be taken as "ground"—illusion-ism, though bellied rock was a belly to them. They did not do cicadas, find annular chitin valuable as design. The muscled stomach in marble becomes back ribs on Cromwell's soldiers, becomes fish. Are you a dorsal or a ventral being. Do you pick up little model cars and turn them over.

In the crystal one sees a woolly red stag, like the one at Trinity all bones one associates not with antlers too large to contemplate, hearing what to Joyce was audible, but knees, massy edible joints, the largest Irish dog, and this must now (not go away but) ribs, all, become joists or shade curved reflection are, that fat thigh, a bottom and knee become single spinal prolongation, the packet of thin but large shells in the fish store, to serve hot deviled crab, tuna eked, combs her hair with an ivory comb, the seductive run of a phrase demanding you put a tail on it, narwhal to keep it from cracking—and in a pharmacy window soak it like ivory nuts in clear oil, and virgins in church panels that look, photographed, like Harlow caringly plump over teeth, are mastodon.

A cicada shell on the lip of a milk bottle must have happened sometime—we all remember frozen necks of cream *and* the thumbnail under leverable up top, our experience of laminate (it would, the semicircle, come up furry, the nail lunate), and on small individual bottles like chef's hats, hammer and peg pegs, the ones that forced the ones ahead through arcane routes to emerge through a hole protected by as it were a nickeled grommet, a Greek clarity of function with mystery at the core. The tiny staple on the milkbottle cap made it a matchbook.

# To Read Away

Here is a list of Einzig Watten Andrews Bernstein Perelman McCaffery Silliman Palmer Hejinian Ward for the August poetics colloquium in Vancouver. My idea of it is people on squarish stuffed chairs in lobbies everywhere, leaning into each other for intensity. Shades at shoulder are Virgil Milton Lucretius Tennyson Coleridge Morris Hopkins who know each other's languages, and Keats for whom they translate. Elementals in desert tents confuse the count; air thickens as lemon Koolaid leaves water gelid. Boatmen off Sirmio: chanty chanty. The colon is mostly it, pause to announce a pause has or is to the associative mind thudding *Maximus,* pulse card out of slot and we remember Olson's beep at who was not Melvilled reprinted small in Kelly and Pack. Any long sentence is Irish, Colin Browne to tuck all into *Writing* that did my two. Stabling but stabilize, they ravined England and Scotland by: defacing statues and excising roofs (rain ruined, word as in Barfield, as globe water dissolves porcelain castles licked senseless as Latin) one could move this parenthesis. Friday I screwed masonite backs to composition shelves covered with plasticized paper teak. Thirty pounds buckle shelves. There's a feel, the hand spreading to separate paperbacks while you insert three or four in a bunch tilted by the other to tuck in cover corner and another, pack of cards in a paper cover the riff or snick, flattening crackers half out of a plastic square tube. Struggle bends, breaks, crumbles. Yet grass and trees distributed Darwin's ways make chancels picturesque. Are the new poetics picturesque. I think yes—shrub growing from the bullet helmet and what a peasant seeing this might think. Continental resentment goes two ways; the knight rather resents the peasant (his daughters fair game as widgeons) and over centuries tales. Earl Gerald's mentioned like a valley all know. It's a stag he comes to with sheep in the tines like brambles. If you've got a cloverleaf mullion or groining in stone you can break it and what's left defines the pattern still. Rhythms educe the ballad, Moynihan's eyes habitually shut in a way that if you were Chesterton would make abbeys rise about you smelling of bread, dogs and laundry as now of turf, smelling just like outside.

# The Line as its Own History

Coleridge saw verse as almost a symptom of what Christopher Fynsk calls "the agitation of the discovery of law," as mystics levitate by less than giving in. Verse isn't a buckling (or hammering of cold metal). The sheep take on, fitfully, the intellectual habits of blue heelers which, awareness of each other readable on brown and grizzled faces, dog as Lahr, show in their shiftiness they see *around* the business of being herded. The moves are not moves, this is not a psychology of "internal-izing." To Morland's lithographic crayon sheep are *nervous* densities. They are prepared to grasp destiny, the slippershaped flower or para-mecium adept. They lay up stores toward recognition.

This mystery is in a verse line as a nervous excitation subsumed by repose, glove in a theater aisle, Yorkshire popovers *left* on a plate, the finding in a public massbook of a card or penciling. A fringe of attention caresses the indented cross (wasn't there, on some St. Josephs, a red embossed one with thorns and lamb? what would feeling this as a color do over time? are there tweeds still lambs?) The lips of any animal muzzle are an introduction to the alien body—not its interior but all of it, as static collects on surfaces. A bowl and cheesecloth ("muslin") make a round pudding. Lamb impaled with mint jelly like holly. Or, art is a goose in moonlight. The world renders itself as odd, at all, Bank of Ireland nothing like of England, the fat pillars different densities, media, like ribbons in a toaster *conduits* for a notion. Reflected in puddles one vanishes.

A metric describing the *failure of nerve* in any given line as its caesura.

The unit is prime. As Kepler looked for mathematicizable planetary intervals a line devolves from verse to prose, a stunning of expectancy. We read looking for that on which to base a felt length; any first line *could* be verse. It is not a hope deferred but a tarnishing. Verse is there first, as objects in a given space give. You can also make cellars from a kind of shale. Eshleman (Silesky says) repairs fractures. Did Poe? Ms. Lee and Ulalume are safely with the angels, though these in him can be randy. Our verse line begins with him, scoffers not observing that any line contains two rates (as Hopkins's undertext will dictate images and more) and it's how to ride this, like Milton's verse unrolled like a carpet, that makes the trouble. Any point in the unrolling is unrolling; there is no point at which how more occurs begins, which means no point at which the poem takes up a relation to temporality. Ricks says it's proleptic. Poe's doubleness, a richness as of weave swearing against color, is like Nin's Golconda volume, narcissism *as* rate, Mexican time (as being assented to) somehow incorporated, the traveler in charge of herself. In these poems Poe lets his instinct run on before, the hound Thoreau lost from his not (acting as if he) knowing a leash is no leash. Well, there's a faith in it, an assuming the pond can be described, its depth in a sense negligible. Poe's verse asserts a uniformity before "Eureka," Lucretian verse made prose.

Today, having just finished *Coleridge the Poet,* I want Silkin on War Poets, Stedman on Romantics and the Portable Matthew Arnold, *Plato and Platonism* and a good clothbound first *Common Reader,* to finish Chesterton's *Chaucer* bought yesterday (in Victor Hugo, which has most of these) and why is this all necessary for my poem on the death of Socrates? I too am all-blending.

So I bought Silkin's *Out of Battle,* and will it give me Troy or Graves, today thinking again of the oddity of As-Shur citadel doors strapped by horizontal beams and ornamental bronze to pinlike poles sunk below the ground, on points, in conical holes in stone, how powdery the grit there, and what beyond metal bands did they have to bind the turning wood? The Science Museum has a butterfly hinge turning circular to linear motion without (the patent pretends) rotation, forgetting the pins working their quarter-circles.

I suppose the gateposts remind me of founding impersonalities, as the phone booth with the gangster inside is walls and a folding door with a spring tense only in transit. The plow turns but interrupts for city gates, so a gate really is not a wall. Can a verse line be a gate? Magic casements, opening on the foam. They don't really get less verse, *become* windows, potted head in Basil. We do clip a nosegay, few fragrants, from our walk (de Sales). It's as if one isn't to see the city door as joinery, any more than you're to imagine yourself sewing seeing brocade (gesturing, seeing Sitwell's rings). The doors are theory rather than practice, soaked in their idea. Then you have studded lines, bossed. Latchet and *louche* hatchet and hooch. It isn't to look newly made, as a doll's house suffers from being new. Yet a line we seem to have always known is not antiqued.

A paragraph as a line gone wrong, indention followed by help-lessness.

"Originality in its narrower sense, as a mere antonym for plagia-rism," John Livingston Lowes says, mind full of quotables as Eliot—

both are period in their taste *for* quote, and the trick was to invent a reason beyond relishing, the quote from desperation, Whan that Aprille gone (not playing) truant in the alleys. And this, as Woolf says breaking off her reviewing of *Love and Freindship,* is all plausible enough and much more might be written in the same strain, rhyming with the samite in grain to the color, nearly, of Philomel's lips—there was a nostalgia for nostalgia to get over. Woolf did it by being matter-of-fact about prunes and custard. Lamb writes about china as sacrificed for. Eliot does not introduce money, as a subject, the way Pound does and this may be a shred of Harvard. The trouble with *humming* the past like a sound is it makes the argument difficult to lift, and I'd say a symptom of Chesterton's importance is how argument as such in his *Chaucer* (almost like assertion in Berdyaev) lifts the matter of Lowes's *Convention and Revolt,* anything to establish a fluidity and this is the value of a verse line, and this does not come merely from the space at beginning and end being more than a fortuity of printing. The drift of the lines in "A Chain for Madeleine" is a drift.

Turner, rightly, never gave a nickel for Ruskin. Call it a farthing. The Petworth studies seen in place in the Tate (especially the Music Party) are infinitely odder than their reproductions. I'd say they are *not* showing that color is shape (as Pound's accents are taken as to be taken as quantities). He renders the mutual reflection of waterfilled globes but not (as Sargent might) the inner light of blue china which in spite of his furriness Vuillard can also get. The undertext here is Whistler's exchanging his collection for a farthing, back as far as my mentioning Lamb in the context of nostalgia and the hard edge money introduces (say in *The Defense of Conny Catching),* the coins so poetical on the cover painting of cards in play, charm in Professor Hoffmann of the offhand naming of "a florin," I suppose from a fleur on earlier forms. As Chesterton revises Lowes on the daisy so the imperfectly round coin squashed with a hammer becomes (given the mint collar) wrappable in a stack in foolscap or hidable under a turned brass cover. A *current* verse line is collared, and this is why World War I poetry is odd, the good and bad about equally. Henry Hay gives a recipe for preparing palming coins to stack without rocking.

# Four Lines Excerpted

Blake's

There is | a mó | ment in | each Dáy | that Sá | tan cán | not find,
Nor cán | his Watch | Fiènds find | it ; | but the | Indús | trious find
This Mo | ment & | it múl | tiplý | & when | it once | is found
It rén | ovates év | ery Mó | ment óf | the Dáy | if right | ly pláced

is not an unfair instance of his long-poem versification. I'd like to say what's significant (given my conservative scansion) is the strong beat on a semicolon. It feels like a thing Blake does often and is measurable, vulnerable to statistical discussion. It is also a question why the eighteenth century's anarchist-poet so often writes verse which in its metric is so flatly ballad or hymn, even nursery-rhyme (everywhere that Mary went). It would be worth knowing how it felt, in the writing, to Blake. Did he fill in the measure as if adding letters (and spaces) on a fixed-length compositor's stick? Or was the richness of internal audibility a kind of filler poured *over* the words, syllables (and, again, their spaces) as concrete over loose stones faced with sand inside a form makes one kind of wall.

Theoretically, reading yards of a long poem should tell you for sure, or nearly for sure, the way (say) Saintsbury will track a Tennyson poem through two stanzas before pronouncing it (almost for convenience) anapestic. A flexible measure, or a measure flexibly handled, increases reader-uncertainty. An ultimately ambiguous measure is an end point, and I'd think would really be a quality of the measured lines, the overall verse strategy, itself. Why, anyway, would the early Romantics condemn Pope's rocking-horse Pegasus and exempt Blake? (Surely this exemption led to the compelling rhythms of Swinburne.)

I once scanned a good stretch of John Ahern's Dante translation as Frostian iambs; he then told me they were syllabics. It was the underline caret (and feeling able to butt two reversed feet, per line) that made the other possible. Acute, grave, light and the caret for nonextant syllable, a syncopated space, were like the Four Elements or humors— nothing you can't explain by some combination, indefeasible. This term, borrowed from Popper, is not praise. An explanatory apparatus that explains all things is suspect; the castle you can't knock down is made of air.

Wimsatt's notion of the paradigm meter, invented really for syllable-stress lines though it should hold for any, raises in pure form the mystery that happens when you take a (the) verse line as the unit. In foot-verse scansion the foot is the unit, inside the line. Four-three ballad measure would (if you're printing it as two lines) give you a two-line "unit"—four if (and I suppose this is Saintsbury's rationale for doubling measures) you don't feel safe until the whole regularity repeats. What makes a *stanza,* then, outside a writer's fiat, is a study indeed. One wants to say the stanza is in no sense a metrical unit, but Spenser is in the way, and Marianne Moore's *Collected Poems.*

These things compel the imagination. It is the notion—even in a sense the perception—of a Line In General that puts an accent on Blake's semicolon. There may be a significant distinction between reading and scanning—a mirror image to Blake's filling out a line without necessarily hearing (or tapping out) Mary had a little lamb. You could argue that the semicolon isn't marked, really, unless you are scanning—phantom blip on the radar screen invisible to the eye. And it would be more interesting to ask what the peculiar (almost prefab) regularity of Blake's measure adds to his meaning. I'd say an expectation that an assertion *will* end at a finite, fairly predictable place. The line will be a phrase, a sense-unit, and a stack of these will be sense.

What scanning does that reading doesn't necessarily do is introduce time, as a moving point with a memory for what has been and some expectations. The reader who scans experiences duration as separable from the poem (as one can read checking syntax, say all the relation-words, in, on, through, back, against). This is to say that scanning is scanning *for* an aspect, but you do alter meaning that way. A poem is different when you've gone through it noting all the color-words. A noun study such as Spurgeon's gives you the illusion of knowing what Shakespeare knew about falconry or law. An absence of physicality may show up as an absence of physical relation-words—for some poets these particles are always metaphorical (used for instance as logical counters, such as subsumption).

And some people are meter-blind, as Wittgenstein knew people he called meaning-blind. There's a sense in which to talk of a reader's "ear" is always absurd, because reductive. You could say the existence of rival scansions, the absurd ones in textbooks, the impatience or rage they rouse, is more than people applying different notions of metrical description. The choice of unit (that inside which comparison occurs) biases results. If your scansions are full of spondees and "weak feet," probably you're letting a line'sworth of stresses crowd into your foot. Acute, grave and light accents are easy to relativise; Joseph Mayor's 0, 1, 2 notation (in *Chapters on English Metre)* forces him to see spondees and so on, from comparing 1s and 2s inside a line, or even over larger areas. So this is also true, that the larger your unit the more an act of scansion tends to crystallize time, rather in the way Stein thought of diagramming as crystallizing a sentence.

Vowels can be slowed by their length, by clustering consonants around them (mouthfilling syllables), by rhyme or at least an adjacent vowel infection, and then by adding a savorable sense. All this is ashes to the clinical scanner, though you need a clean (even a sterile) scansion to build comment on.

This piece could have the same number of words in each paragraph, and nobody would notice because nobody would care. Since metrical regularity is distributed over a larger repeating unit (the line) it alters time, felt as reading rate and rhythmic units (basically a horizontal unit *becoming vertical,* for written verse—oral epics may feel more like visiting the same place altered by weather or number of goats), or might be said to give words a memory of each other. For this reason, metaphor though we're in, it really does matter even to the unsophisticated reader how *transparent* Blake's meter was to him. We all remember the slow-motion scansion that makes "Poison Tree" depend on its colons. Williams's "Poem" about cat and jamcloset has been exhibited as its line-breaks. This is slow motion, figuring out bird flight from freeze frames. You might better ask, thinking again of paradigm meter, what alterations could I make in these paragraphs, or sentences, to make them "metrical," and at what point then does doing that change, merely from a shift in attention, their existence, as print, in time.

It involves a feeling that one *can* read backwards, possibly that one is. Squeals of brakes are as if to repair an error of judgment; though acknowledging the past they also wish to alter it. Listening can be retrospective. A paradigmatic line is raised as a specter, the rose behind the rose, but also as a ruler, a prospective tool. It looks for things to extend to or annex, as a compass's ideal circle is made with it flat out the point horizontal to the paper, its puncture notional. Or the line as cone has its own paradigm, excluding the penumbra. The model pitches me forward, yet in actually reading metered verse I feel where I am, liking to be there as if a peasant with an idea of degree. To be *in* meter is like being in a metaphor. Wine on the table in a grapegrown pergola is neither in nor out. Is being in a meter more like being in a fit or being in debt? This kind of question can at least be asked.

"Moment . . . Day . . . Satan . . . find," the stressed words in Blake's line, occur at metrically sensitive points—breaks between feet, a line end. This may be his counterpoint, in his head, important words at important places (more like Pope than Creeley). Words as sense-heightened units may be the issue with him. It feels to me, now that I'm selecting for it, like grave and acute stresses clustering; I think it's these his eye would check, and his nonsense hero-names may be similarly modular. That would make sense, a regular meter to be got away from in ways not strictly metrical, invisible to civilized scansion. It's what Dickinson may be said to be doing as well, using traditional rhythmic accents to isolate important words, usually rhymed. Blake's find-find-found line ends are similarly broadvoweled. Sense and the phrase end coincide.

The urge to quibble clusters around Blake's semicolon. Given the semiambiguous *activity* of scanning (since it's hard or impossible to make all the principles explicit), and ambiguous rhythms in lines which don't by nature sprout or secrete bars, no wonder a difference is so readily felt as error.

Generations were beaten for making false quantities. We could take the rough and readiness of Blake's epic line as folk revolt (lumping the ballads with Ossian) or keeping something invested in regularity. Perhaps the question to ask is why Blake's line, Miltonic matter without the baggage, Orientalia, clustered stresses, contorted sense, is not in its clarity more wooden.

The penultimately accented line ends in Clough's *Bothie* are read as sense units, though the genius of the language as Saintsbury would say, especially if we weren't thinking of classical foot-shapes as possible in English, would have us enclose the final syllable in a parenthesis, and scan it with the first syllable of the line after as an iamb:

> When the armies are set in array, and the battle beginning,
> Is it well that the soldier whose post is far to the leftward
> Say, I will go to the right, it is there I shall do best service?
> There is a great Field-Marshal, my friend, who arrays our batallions;
> Let us to Providence trust, and abide and work in our stations.

His sense of the world for me is thin but welcome; he does wonder that what is in it is in it. Greek and porridge, and the meter is I think deliberately intrusive, felt as a frame as we try to stretch final disyllables to spondees. At any rate, beginning so many lines with a stress is hardly possible without the feminine fall at the end; the last syllable drones because really between two meters. Blake on the other hand begins lines with fairly strong words which the meter reduces to less than the syllable after. What we *can* read Blake's lines as, a kind of prosy doggerel, Clough's matter (by outprosing the metric clatter) evades. Blake's lines printed as prose would sound like a Dryden preface. Browne's *Cyrus:*

> As for the delights, commodities, mysteries, with other
> Concernments of this order, we are unwilling to fly them over,
> In the short deliveries of Virgil, Varro, or others,
> And shall therefore enlarge with additional ampliations.

This is *like* Clough, we think, as any prose after the razzle-dazzle of an ambiguous measure will seem, for a while, to fit. Perhaps there is a hexameter length that stays with you, from the classroom.

Yet the law is not convenience. It's not just the disappointing cases that make it hard to scan *The Garden of Cyrus* through. Done it would be a curio as Clough's lines are in a way curios. One way Blake is disarming is by not being up to that. Time in his verse does not include classicist vistas (one line in *Bothie* is, predictably, "Aeschylus, Sophocles, Homer, Herodotus, Pindar, and Plato.") It matters in both that you are in the middle of a great many lines like that. A serious long poem's measure in a sense never starts, and this is a way the paradigm line is not prospective. I felt Williams's "This Is Just to Say" could be rewritten in hexameters; that it wouldn't quite go is his wariness. When Milton nods it's often by enjambing two and three-beat phrases in mechanical alternation so that, beginning in the middle of a line, you can rebreak a long stretch before hitting an anomaly.

Seven-beat lines tend to collapse (especially given a high percentage of monosyllables) into strong-stress fours. Blake's do, and I think in the reading for once this is not a sign of slack writing. It happens when every other foot is "weak," and this may be deliberate since the syllables of four important words are about all that length of line can take, as in a five-beat line two or three "important" words tend to be maximum. It is an ongoing thing you fill. A paradigmatic line may say little about how an actual line decides to go on; building that hesitation in at the end (as more than a statistical remark) would be curious. A line is not merely the sum of its measure *or* a duration felt to be equivalent to another line, though we would gain if people wrote verse a while in lines merely *felt* to be equal. Kenneth Irby's long lines in "A Set" may emancipate as the camera freed the painters; any lines shorter than his are equal.

Does a paradigm meter hover over the first line of a poem? if we start in the middle or browse backward? Meter's vertical dimension annihilates time, and in so doing annihilates beginning. We are always reading a long poem; any browsing is automatically reading *in.* This may be like the metaphor's complicity, that to understand it is to enact it. Similarly a line or two quoted out of context aren't "really" isolated. It's the last line that surprises, by being (no matter how boffo) so flat. Meter will flatten, partly by absorbing all (Sir Thomas Browne to Clough) to it. I found this Blake quoted in Harold Brooks on *Four Quartets,* and it secreted this out of its superfluity—really as a by-product of the act of scanning it.

# A Swinburne Reliquary

> Night, a black hound, follows the white fawn day,
> Sorrow had filled her shaken eyelids' blue
> But see now, Lord; her mouth is lovelier.
> I had grown pure as the dawn and the dew,
> Bound with her myrtles, beaten with her rods,
> They are merciful, clothed with pity, the
> > young compassionate Gods.
> Choose of two loves and cleave unto the best,
> Wine and rank poison, milk and blood,
> Love bites and stings me through, to see
> Through the kisses that blossom and bud,
> With tender blood, and colour of your throat,
> We are vexed and cumbered in earth's sight
> In the month of the long decline of roses
> Too wan for blushing and too warm for white,
> The sacred body hangs and bleeds.
> Till the hour shall bid them climb
> Where stingless pleasure has no foam or fang
> I send my love back to the lovely time.

The situations and verbs in Swinburne are mostly generic, much-fingered coins. Each line above is from a different one of his poems. What is this but to say that words are for him part of utterance, not part of experience. As if to say a poem by him is a kind of behavior. This may be more honest than a deliberate confusion of word with thing but it's odd that, deliquescing into song, he found so many admirers, so broad a public, among people we think of as liking heavy furniture.

So the temptation is to take him as some kind of type, as Shelley became an emblem for many, though he and (say) Wordsworth are so different one wonders they had readers in common. Swinburne was "musical," though Welby's *Study* prefers "metrical," arguing that individual words are subjugated to a beat. Yet it's too easy to think of marching rhythms as an antidote to idyll-sounds, undulations of indoor vowels. What I miss always, to the point of wondering if Darwin weren't ironic when he complained of having lost all poetic sense, is not the particular as such, or any kind of speciation, as much as an attitude (perhaps like Gilbert White's) that value lies in the particular, that the specific is idiosyncratic, and then a sense of relatedness, as that earthworms have a job. Darwin, with that sense of humor and those attacks of weakness, may have been odd but hardly unpoetic. The problems he attacks are too difficult to resolve into a kind of engineering. He had files, and his furniture was heavy (and his lab equipment often makeshift. His habit of seeing household items as apparatus is part of his sense of process.) I can't but see it as different—compare Dickens taking walks at night, observing—from whatever it was that moved Swinburne, even if a rhythm, to the tool he makes.

I've been killing large cockroaches lately by bashing them. It's like killing dogs.

Darwin is praised for giving full value to the *slight* discrepancy—and of course having no shame at all in making up hypotheses to explain it. Is this boring yet. Say that what Swinburne did—however he did it—was more expressive than investigative. Just as Beckett seems overconcerned with commonplace psychological motions, a latter-day Dickens, no. It is that Swinburne deals by definition with interchangeable contexts.

The large roach is new. My house is so poisoned that invaders tend to be single. These are each solitary but several. They have just enough bulk or their bulk in relation to their rate is such that hesitations are mammalian or deliberate. I remember once in the old parent Half-Price Books disturbing a lower shelf and large ones came scrabbling out of the *spines* of books.

Yet we can take *Atalanta,* the to-do, almost as full of objects as Ben Jonson, a culture imagined expressing itself in terms of objects, gone ritual, as Jonson's domestic lists are objects or middleclass wealth gone mad, something of the humor Max Apple finds in naming anything recognizable. Scriptural or Blakean *Erechtheus,* something *odd* in the pother, dissolving felt to imagined fact, then "Thalassius," bit of Whitman infused but too *much* verse too imagined, the fact gone imagination's way. There's a boar in *Atalanta,* and love for the killing of it. This, by the way, is the Althea of whom Shakespeare made the burning-brand jokes.

> And I with gathered raiment from the bed
> Sprang, and drew forth the brand, and cast on it
> Water, and trod the flame bare-foot, and crushed
> With naked hand spark beaten out of spark
> And blew against and quenched it;

the technique and imagining ("with gathered raiment") Elizabethan, but what do we know, the sound already loss, lost Greek. Beginning of literary archeology, imagining writing about Virgil eating.

Bleacher verse or bleached; even the spilt blood is somehow silvery. The insides of burst roaches include pale bits, like meal.

> I found in dreams a place of wind and flowers,
>> Full of sweet trees and colour of glad grass,
>> In midst whereof there was

and you get a lady like Creeley's "Kore." Grass, if you paint, is many colors, many species. So I'm questioning not a sloppiness but the *value* of what is unlikely to be surprised. And yet we're glad that the color of grass is glad, grass is. All of it may be mental pastoral, codes or signals so one need not say carved of bowl, then reject bowl—not on grounds of, how else does he eat the curds, of common sense milieu. More a convention that what's fitting may be imagined as here.

Glasses that run are hourglasses, emblems without physicality, transparent lambs, glass bears eating prophets or philosophers. If the world were transparent it would merely be practical. The right diet turns termites transparent, lovely globby glass things, so why not emblems like heaped weapons?

Gadamer, Saturn of the wandering seven, has no place for multiple contexts rarefied to ideality, so that any "general" word alludes to a way of being. Swinburne's, unlike Wittgenstein's workers with their bits of board, almost never contain the practical. So "sorrow," never "misery" except maybe in the plays, is not a state but a character, as a singer one sees in *Carmina Burana* may or may not be singing that minute. Well, we may have regressed to think of mental events as vulnerable to technique, practicality. But without the practical what becomes of the urgent.

Do we *need* the urgent, in verse which looks so romantic? We may have samples, words on a page no longer to be sung, like a Sarum breviary. His few bits of bone or hair may always have been this, and was it then an excuse to caress the amethyst? When I was young we really weren't to touch the blessed utensils, tabu. Just maybe having no Greek makes us unable to *handle* his or perceive the handling but I don't think so. He thinks in a different key when he writes verse, and thinks of it as "song." Print him like a missal, with red bits.

My own Latin is gone. But this *won't* be like coming not to be able to read Swinburne. His chanters didn't care if the sense were going to vapor. The meter was like Latin consonants, chanted or sung, bite of an obvious discipline. His lines are to be found printed on the menus, not steaming on the plate.

It would be interesting if meter alone denies him a place with nonreferential poetry. Of rhythm there is a construct or something. So repeating rhythm is vulgar now, like a steamed turbot. How far we've come from him demands his collaboration, as his Bible allusions in odd places, the rectory clutter, undercut impiety. Fashion is not the question; his notion of "poetry" as adopted was popular but not central.

So now he's a sect like people who drink to the Stuarts or hate fluorine. Lacking poison or alcohol to throw at roaches, try boiling water. I was thinking that the magician's sense of my card, what was your card, is like the possessive one's tea, I haven't had my tea. Swinburne's going inside his head for subject and illustration, in outgoing if not outdoor measures, lets him say "my verse" or my decorations on the pot. Wind and rain in the tea.

# Stepped Indention as a Halfway Measure

The time has come to say something of Williams's "variable foot." Harvey Gross (*Sound and Form in Modern Poetry*) says Whitman's lolloping long lines tend to be perceived as equivalent, merely from their being lines. The Standard Variable in Williams is three short lines, the last two progressively stepped with a hefty indention as if the electrical typewriter the hospital gave him has a tractable tab key.

> In our family we stammer unless,
> > half mad,
> > > we come to speech at last

Runover lines are flush with their indention.

Williams thought of the three-line bloc as a line, made up of three "feet." How can he get away with this, when foot-prosody traditionally involves a repeating, pretty well fixed pattern of syllables in time (Gross's "syllable stress," iambs or trochees glacéed into a bar like music), or a major whack among others, relative to each other, the number (per line) fixed—"strong stress," not a timed measure. Eliot's "April is the cruelest month" is strong-stress fours, though in *Lucifer in Harness* Fussell once tried to scan it the other way. Albert Cook's *The Classic Line* gives you a rule: any line not by Milton will have one foor with a major*est* stress, gauged relative to the other heavy beats in that line. Gross has a rule (for scanning inverted feet, that sloppy critics too easily call spondees, or weak feet they give two light stresses), that one assigns weights to the syllables in a foot relative to each other *only* inside the foot.

In short, meter will throw you unless you stipulate what you're measuring *relative to what,* and keep that unit *short.* This doesn't handle syllabics, like Marianne Moore's, but those you just read and be pleased. What have these to do with *indention?* In theory, nothing. An indented line is indented relative to another line; in this sense it is a *vertical* dimension, and feet are horizontal. Further, the free-verse convention is to indent for a pause—or indent whole sections, as in the *Maximus* poems, like an outline (this might be called *parenthetical* indention). Williams gets *some* pause or parenthetical-afterthought mileage out of his steps, but in general that's not what they're for. The forty years before he often spaced short (and short-line) poems in three-line groups, sometimes four. In the good poems these mini-stanzas break in the middle of sense-units, so the mini-stanza breaks are syntactical caesurae. Note that the variable feet can function like a reminder to do likewise, *because they are stepped* and hence give more the ongoing feel of a single line.

That is in fact the test. If you're wondering why a bad middle-period Williams poem is bad, look at the stanza breaks; if they correspond with sense-units it's a sign his energy failed him. (Creeley would later build a metric from this line-end violence, taking straight off from Williams.) For variable feet, imagine them printed flush left as a middle-Williams tercet—if the lines lose nothing, he's coasting.

Mary Oliver's *Twelve Moons* includes two stepped poems, both about seacoasts, and they're hard to quote a *little* of because her left-margin lines are sentence-middles. Here is about half of "Mussels":

> In the riprap,
>     in the cool caves,
>         in the dim and salt-refreshed
>             recesses, they cling
>     [. . .] At low tide
>         I am on the riprap, clattering
>             with boots and a pail,
> rock over rock; I choose
>     the crevice, I reach
>         forward into the dampness,
>             my hands feeling everywhere
> for the best, the biggest. Even before
>     I decide which to take,
>         which to twist from the wet rocks,
>             which to devour,
> they, who have no eyes to see with,
>     see me, like a shadow,
>         bending forward. Together
>             they make a sound,
> not loud,
>     not unmusical, as they lean
>         into the rocks, away
>             from my grasping fingers.

What struck me when I picked up this book was how bad this would be flush left. In fact, starting from "At low tide" you could rewrite each group of four as two five-beat lines, but I mention this only to show that a certain old-fashionedness in her will out. By contrast, Williams's triples do tend to make more of a line. Oliver's poem is almost a diorama of step-indention, experience glued by metrical *rate* into one ball.

Williams's handling counts as a *measure* in ways hers does not. Perhaps three is the limit for indention to be a "line," Gross's rule to apply in little, and the stacked three felt as equivalent (each a "beat," say.) I once asked Bob Trammell how a poet could, reading aloud, signal indentions (I was thinking of block indentions.) After a wait I said "Well?" and he said, "I just did." Listening to recorded Williams shows how different he is from Creeley—how little in *saying* a poem he is stopped by line ends and starts. So he was temperamentally inclined to see stepped lines as one line. All this works together and the question is does it make a, properly speaking, *metrical* innovation, if "measure" is the disposal of patent regularities, though Williams was so fond of stressing "variable." I think it does, by way of Gross's remark about long lines felt as equivalent, and you compare the triplets to each other inside the triplet, more as if each line were a syllable in a foot than if each is a foot in a three-foot "line" broken vertically. The step-relation is that intimate.

# Indention as Intention in *Maximus I*

What they teach in poetry courses may not be much help with Olson. Leafing through *The Maximus Poems* it's easy to find the multiply indented "History is the Memory of Time" lyric enough. It gives us the historical background we need for the "fish rush" and Stage Fight,

> when she must have been a cowtown from the roar
> of men after, fish:

followed by an indention for conjecture, guessing the number of fishermen in port by guessing the number of ships. The descriptions of Standish and the hogshead barricade are efficient the way good cinema cutting is, glimpses when glimpses will serve, then a flash (indented) to the competition vessels, sketched in as these later Vol. I *Maximus* poems tend to be from records. The feeling is for the reader of a man feeling his way back into history, putting the meaning back into events starkly (if anecdotally) rendered in what you might call the Protestant Relations. True in a way to this, to Tawney, as much as infection from Pound, the poem ends in a step-like series (stages?) on what cash not credit, "real bucks," were to the Gloucestermen, modulating into an attack on "conantry" and "mutual losing banks," then back to the margin with what is almost a marginal illustration—the imagined monument (historically imagined),

> to a fisherman crouched down
> behind a hogshead, protecting
> his dried fish

which ending completes the five-poem suite begun in "Letter 23." It is a feat worth applauding that the poems contain so much information without sounding like Historical Society minutes. Everything gets used again. The self-regard of the earlier poems, on Olson's *place* in Gloucester and what largeness is left, is there in the remarks on Pindar and Herodotus, mem-o-ry (a glance at the popular song and *memoria)* and the marveling that places *he* knew *they* knew, summed up (in "Maximus to Gloucester") in the point-of-view reversed metaphor,

> (like backwards
> of a scene
> I saw the other way
> for thirty years)
>
> Gloucester can view
> those men
> who saw her
> first

which turns what he does in these poems from the merely personal to (the subject is) an exercise of the historical imagination. Olson *happens* to be interested because of what *happens* to impinge on him now (Stage Head, the Cut), but he knows very well from Pound that epic may be contained in the local—vision is possible sitting on the Dogana steps—and from Melville that facts properly laid down are cargo. All this, because of tactical placement in a short stretch, animates that terminal vignette beginning "They should raise a monument" and ending with the historical possessive "his dried fish."

The next five poems, "The Picture" through "Capt Christopher Levett (of York)" seem wanting to add, in a series of retakes, the history of Europe as an overlay, which implicates this set in a kind of *historismus.* The indentions become *tabular* in intent, the poems anatomies, Gloucester Display'd. These are, as a set, much harder to read because they assume in the reader kinds of commitment to history for its own sake, say history as self-justifying. "The Picture'"s subsection, called THE PICTURE: with caps and colon, is a table by date of voyages with sketched cargo, livened a bit by three-beat endings: "John Watts factor?" "left Stage Head" "Watts took salt." Then we get to Weymouth Port Book research, a thirty-four item list like something out of *Crusoe,* and a deliberately muffled ending (on an "etc.") And no indentions till "1st Letter on Georges" and the Second Letter's double column. It would be interesting to know if for that stretch, from "Some Good News" to "Capt Christopher Levett (of York)" Olson tired of indention or regarded these three as totally digested, each one thing in its linearity. The cinema, explicit at the end of "The Picture," gives way to historical pemmican. We remain in the "objectivity" of collaged report until the very important ending to "John Burke," in which inside and outside are dismissed in favor of the topological stance adumbrated in "Equal, That Is." I think an anxiety about the place in poetry of historic assertion evaporates, right here with

> ". . . being Fosterwise of
> Charley-once-boy
> insides"

making possible the map and sounding transcriptions of "Letter, May 2, 1959" in which (once more with indentions) he writes *inside* of history as he once wrote "in" a thicket. "In Cold Hell" raises the possibility of being "in" a medieval metaphor, as the last poems in the first *Maximus* volume come to an understanding of history in the historical poem as co-presence, so that words transcribed from documents are at the end no more transcribed than Olson's own words, the poem a fascicle—longitudinal knot—held together by mutual abrasion, a common abrasiveness.

# How Olson Does Impress

I know of few books of criticism like Albert Cook's *The Classic Line,* which consider the sort of line-in-general of some very good poets in terms of how much weight and what kind it's designed to carry. Surely that and some syntactical dodges from Davie's *Articulate Energy* are what is required to talk about Olson's significance as (if we must) a post-modern writer, especially his significance for other writers. Yet the bulk of Olson criticism in print is the same old description as explanation, this line means this thing.

A poet talking about other poets is usually talking about himself, and Olson's preference for late Pound-prose to late Pound-verse may have a reflexive arm. My own belief is that, while the good *Human Universe* prose wears very well, the good verse is even better, say everything in *In Cold Hell, In Thicket,* and the first twenty or so *Maximus* poems; after that the more he explains the worse the verse gets. His decline (as if every good poet after Wordsworth were condemned to follow his curve) is like Williams's and maybe like Pound's, only more interesting—because a good quarter of his critical energy went into being very clear why American long poems fail. But that failure, which is everywhere in the second set of Maximi, is in the line, and good descriptive criticism should start off saying so.

After all, his theory *as* theory reduces to a neo-Spenglerian puttering about with hiply nonwestern cultures, as objects his Lawrencian vitalism could caress. His *good* theory is about line and syllable as spoke, and doesn't need a Greek dictionary. There, in "Projective Verse" and *Letters for Origin,* and the Pound bits in *Mayan Letters,* he's as intelligent as Gertrude Stein in *Narration* and *Geographical History of America* on why modern narrative is dull and where the good stuff comes from. The culture whuff seems a hankering after size in the old manner, and the string of fathers (Melville-Dahlberg-Pound-himself) a coarse quest for a power-source. Critics are already writing off Dahlberg's remark that he stopped reading Olson in the mid-fifties when he stopped writing English as the bitterness of one betrayed by a disciple. One trouble there is that Dahlberg has no idea what a verse line is *for,** so can hardly be expected to applaud good things in *Cold Hell* and *Maximus*.

Consider their prose. Dahlberg's is designed firstly to remind you of his favorite Renaissance writers, their leafy and meaty substance, but in form is consciously old-fashioned as they were not, as if to say these values are dead but look, they're alive here. *Priapus* pays me back more than *Because I Was Flesh,* but in that book his line, so to speak, is also a vehicle to contain any amount of pain he chooses to put in. Personal pain, that is, as if he has become Job. What Cook says is that the great poets come up with a verse line to contain everybody's pain—like the author of *Job.*

Now the first characteristic of Olson's prose and verse is energy—and I suppose that's enough to make him the enemy of flaccid versifiers in little magazines. The second is an admirable tendency to take risks. Apparently her broke into his best stuff by a kind of Action Writing, which is why he found Dahlberg's injunction to keep it moving so helpful, though Dahlberg will have meant it for his own problem in *Priapus,* which is what to say next when your subject is a *theme* (food, plants, lust).

But if Cook were tasting Olson's line, the first thing he'd say is that it's designed to report results, forcefully. This means that the prose as prose and verse as line is not principally an investigative tool, however much in the writing he may turn it into one. Think of "Human Universe," "Equal, That Is," or any of the good *Maximus* poems and it's clear that though designed to stay alive, which is what art is for, they make as if to say things (certainties, facts) otherwise got at. After all, even when one of the great essays came all in a chunk, it's things he's been thinking *over* for a long time. The problem in the essays, and for any art involving thought, is how to render thought thinking rather than Thought Thunk, as the French would say. He solves it better in the performance essays than in the reviews. In verse, the best of the "thinking" is what Marcel (say) would call mythic, muddling around where the mysteries are. But most good readers I know agree that when he starts recording documents (thanking Pound for rag-bag), and later thinks that naming *old* myths (Tiamat, etc.) helps, the line goes irretrievably dead.

When he talks about the *intimate* parts of writing (line-lengths are emotional and syllables are not, as if paraphrasing Stein) the

---

*He once suggested, blandly, that I turn a little poem of mine into prose for a market he had in mind, and is always willing to turn his own prose into verse. He finds my objections effete.

verse line is just fine. But he did get to like the sound of himself explaining, and the explaining-sound is dead if that's all there is.

Williams's very helpful double-Bill on Pound in a late *Massachu-setts Review* says he can put damn near anything in a poem because he times it on the way down. It's why his gnomic scraps don't offend more, certainly. But Olson's theorizing led him into something oddly like Pound's position, that a good long poem takes research—especially historical—and we end up by way of Herodotus in document-collage. What he's *good* at, we'd say, is firsthand stuff so completely digested he doesn't know it's there until it gets into his poem.

I'm trying hard to stay off the question of why he chose to make cosmic assertions. Probably the magnetic influence of Pound (or the *idea* of Pound), and that consequence of a taste for size that models become heroes. Or perhaps wanting size should never be a taste, but a settled expectation. No epic hero knows he is, and you don't get epic size by trying not to know. Vitalism says you can, which is why it too is a dead end.

He writes with thick wrists. He is hopelessly sexist for more reasons than men and girls, and all the triste lines about how hard it is for we awkward men to be graceful may be built around a lie—we expect he could be graceful whenever he chose. I mention this because it's there in the line, that huffy, troll-under-a-bridge manner, that I expect repels academic readers who endure it for what they can say about his matter. When MacDiarmid did it in a long poem he pretended to be drunk.

Yet that push-push-push, as if Creeley's line-breaks become com-mas, *is* powerful and does box him in as it were, to need to say something wonderful to come up to his beginnings. It also manages to be dignified, and he did like verse to be *heightened* that way.

The commas make a resistant medium—so he can mime plain man coming at hard truths—and make it possible to build by accretion, what luck and a trained back brain let come to him. He had the hesitation-pitch down so early it's doubly wonderful he dropped it in later Maximi, without replacing it with an equally powerful device. Maybe from wishful thinking he thought he too could get away with *Tempest*-pure plain statement. Of course the first thing a *danced* difficulty does is turn your poem into an event, a performance, and this is going to look like Pound's self-mythization though he found it earlier in Melville, who is always willing to talk about what he'd like to do next.

But this standard move, poet as Exemplary Man coming at what matters, is hardly what matters in the verse, and for Olson may have been a strategic mistake. It's easy to escape old-fashioned humanism by sinking below it to mere particulars, and Self as Narrative is Wordsworth one more time; at least it can be asked in what sense Olson's isn't. What makes the verse wonderful is just what he said did, intelligent syllables and passionate line-breaks. The matter stays what happens to matter to Olson, except insofar as these make it mean more. If he'd been patient and made more of it, *Maximus* would certainly be a wonderful long thing. As is, once past the ranting vestibule it's the best *start* an American long poem has had since Canto I (suggesting as it does a direction only by the higher hindsight).

There must be a way to say this. Olson is a good poet because he fiddled with rate (and only then, with rhythm) in ways that made his lines more *deliberate* than anyone else's—except Creeley's in shorter things—and what is signaled as deliberate is taken as more meant. His job then was to find things to mean.

The country—well. Why not. A good bet since Juvenal. The village—as a way in to people and the little ethic of how to be human though oneself (in spite of one's neighbors). He made it hard not to preach, but insofar as he made good things he preached well. What he wanted in the line I should say was a mixture of utter sincerity, grandeur and intimacy. Hence the huffy Maximus, but Letters of. What matters in the verse is that he did it.

That his *un*conscious sillinesses are pure gain in that line may be an argument against it (here's my cod—who will lift it?), but who else, trying, has, as much. Stein in the think-pieces, *Geographical History,* but not in a big art-thing as such. She also distressed the line until every word was signaled as deliberate. That was the job the Modernists (Moore and Stevens too) gave themselves. All of them have trouble with Subjects (one of their virtues is that subject *is* a trouble to them), and all of them—except Williams—write best about writing. According to these, Olson counts as the last of the Modernists. What makes him more, I think, is partly his trying to assimilate their advances—consolidate their gains—while writing things as close to ordinary as he could.

For a year I've been wondering why it's so hard to wash little cockroaches down the sink, and lately it struck me it may be for the reason Poe uses in "Maelstrom." If that got in an Olson poem, the line would be as hospitable to the cockroach (or toilet-ball, etc.) as to the formula. When Pound does that he'll either inflate it (the ant's a centaur) or fall into anti-lyric decorum. Olson can always write about what happens to impinge (landscape, in "Cold Hell"; weather reports in *Maximus)* without condescension, and at best without a this matters *because* here-now.

Another way to say it is that while everybody talks about his height, few mention his weight. The inertial mass of him comes through in the line, and he can talk about little things without having to unbend or apologize.

Scale is peculiar. If a building were two sizes larger it would be the same building only bigger. What's a bigger subject, and how do words say themselves large. Not by talking big. My Olson's at the binder but I go through him in my head. There is firstly the waterhead of everything you leave out—hence the spare power of "Tyrian Businesses" (which sings in everybody's head, and in the short openings is a Zukofskyan Test of the difference between Creeley and Olson). Then there's the trouble with that declarative stance. Maximus is fond of maxims, which Aristotle says in the *Rhetoric* don't touch till you're forty. It's why Sancho is funny but also because peasants don't teach gentry. One gentle joke in *Maximus* is that one does. The trouble with maxims is that they're common-places, topoi indeed, and that may be in *Maximus* a useful flattening, as it is important in Dahlberg's *Priapus* that you know it all already. Helps elevate texture.

Again there's that hieratic (legal?) putting do in everywhere; they do move. The earth do. As if half-remembered highschool Latin. Maximus, Charlie-praetor-once-was, is a stylistic imperialist who conquers by doing—by being able to say at all. The wrestling mat as a map of colored light? One thing that makes it more than one soul's voyage is that he conquers this and that for other writers— and only then for other readers—in a diminished time. The effort weas to take it as not. And then there was relation.

A short history of philosophy. Plato: what's the essence of? Galileo: what's the relation between. And then Wittgenstein, whose grace is to attack a problem from all sides at once (a contracting spherical wave front) without knowing what the problem is. It's a beautiful instinct, and makes philosophy more like hunting. It doesn't matter that he sold it as piecework.

Spengler shorthands relation as mathematical function, and this has nothing much to do with Olson except that he cared about bodies (in their mass, more than relative rates), especially human bodies, as if an existential physics were possible. Grace matters not as analogue to a proof's elegance, but as a symptom of dignity which he'd like to make a part of mass.

Which if this were a metaphor-chain would bring us to *the* Mass, but even his references to the Virgin are secular. If anything, you could say his achievement caps a nineteenth-century wish, and he sacralizes things without making them holy.

What the verse does as chant is make things important without changing them. Chant rather than blessing. God has nothing much to do in his system, except look at all the other gods. Or he's a closet worshipper, as in the Pastoral Letter. He won't, then, plug into deity for size, though one feels he'd like to wrestle God.

Here again it's the line that does it, has it to do. He will attack and celebrate rather than mention—there's more bustle that way. Remarks are recognized, which is why they are not literature, and the process in Olson poems is the process of reading them. You learn to read Olson by intuiting a rule of recognition, and his signals come at you from any direction. This is fun but also engages you, so that what you recognize stays read. One does collaborate.

# Magic in Verse—Some Distinctions

I'm reading Longfellow's "The Jewish Cemetery at Newport" in Rodman's collection and see (how easily the first stanzas go down) that Poe's calling him a plagiarist made sense, had a deep resonance to it. His quondam gothic may be in an odd relation to time, as Watson argues Coleridge was—hobnobbing with the pastness of the past without the work of history, what we've come to think of as its Blue Book, slum statistic quality. History floats free in their poems. But Longfellow is familiar with history, it's his, like friends at a costume party so we don't mind modern plaster tinted, in him. Poe reminds you that the Funhouse has depths. It will never get out of hand in Longfellow and at the end of his poem he buries the dead. Everything is what you thought it was. This is the plaster statue on the mantel, Greece recaptured. A raven on one is a risk. Jeffers's "Hellenistics" in the same volume pretends we could have had Greek perceptions all along—it's just stuff, little cakes, Hebraistics. That's why the line about having wasted his life, in that Wright poem.

> The foam-heads, the exultant dawn light going
> > west, the pelicans, their huge wings
> > half folded, plunging like stones.

> And these sepulchral stones, so old and brown,
> > That pave with level flags their burial-place,
> Seem like the tablets of the Law, thrown down
> > And broken by Moses at the mountain's base.

Plagiary pits inherit against earn or appropriate, and how to say this unsmarmily is a problem. There's the generosity of Poe, picking through a book of verse for good lines, anything to raise a tremor even in the intellect. Just today I'm told there's a *chance* the sixteen-year-old deserter was walled up (in his uniform) while Edgar A. Perry was enlisted, on the island off Boston. The sudden jolt, to think he *might* have collaborated (at least by silence) in an action we'd bracketed as invention is like seeing one's wife in a new aspect. The possibility of new relations of life and art is there in Poe. A jeweler's window I pass weeks apart just down from the Parker House where Dickens stayed has on display a large plain gold ring surmounted by an ivory skull facing forward rather than out (as it does in potmetal ones with ruby eyes), the sutures well indicated in brown not wholly stain. It would be a good command charm; Yeats might have used it with a dagger to cut air, stamping his foot for punctuation. The ring reminds you of lore as preliminary to action. The imagination of it involves will. I don't approve of will in spells and have thought of it as bracketed (or thought of spells as a choice neither involving nor not involving will). Usually it's fuzzed; will somehow enters heavy picturing as doggedness, the clenching of one's picturemaking teeth. Or it's a sending (spatial, spatial) of a mental gesture analogous to urging the golf or croquet ball on its way, corrective intent as vector. Part of my trouble with this is its wanting to play ball with causal description, inserting the thin edge of wish into physics. Yesterday I wondered a second whether an arcane connection could be demonstrated between imagination and will, by pointing to the frequency of will, concentration, focus metaphors in nearly any description of contemporary magic.

Today I'm considering stone in Longfellow and Jeffers, whose stones are bits of cliffs and I think not very carvable. Probably both find it natural that stones will crack, not a very classical viewpoint (Williams's saxifrage, "my flower that splits/the rocks.") Stone is a victim of cold. In Poe, however crumbled the mortar, stone inhabits a literary space, and this is what the discovery of the body walled in invades. Longfellow leaves everything as he found it, the assemblage pleasant, a Cotton Club (revived here the 31st in Copley Square). The Athenaeum guard said Eve's despondent because she looked under Adam's figleaf and found nothing. From this it's not so far to the vulgarity of the Pygmalion statue half gray half rosy, the sculptor kissing it like Sarasate bent backwards.

There's nothing, not even a glacier, you couldn't put in your living room. Tissot is proof that everything is domestic. By contrast I would say that magic occurs between leaves in a forest where no one sees, that lichen mutter, unthinkably woody, and the cabochon gem is proof that nature is unwitting. The veins when a leaf rots are not really like a screen door, nor are they pretty. A record, history is not pretty. So nothing that is read is—even De Quincey's prose is not like our first view of Strawberry Hill.

"Notes on a Visit to Le Tuc d'Audoubert" impressed me (read by Eshleman in Dallas after slides) as enactment, the sections (verse, prose—and *drawings,* how do you read drawings) discovery, travels with a bison, dense, believable. I think he'll prefer in a way, as an act of mind, "Visions of the Fathers of Lascaux," though the trappings of this are to me like Williams's ovum and sperm book cover, things surprised to find themselves design.

There is a Romantic question here, whether the license to preach is an issue in this verse, whether we need find Eshleman believable to believe him. He suffers an expansion of "the so-called Whore/on her severely underfed Dragon" (I suppose a medieval representation in stone) and it's believable that having seen it he votes for the concept *of* it. He finds, or observes, a deliberate confusion of these in him almost constituting vision, "that fresh rain air is a clear indication/that here is not entirely here." Usually I prefer his here poems, even if here is memory ("Still-Life with Fraternity") or straight dream-vision ("Fathers of Lascaux"), but a virtue of his poetry is reconciling me to a mixture, the slug in "Name Encanyoned River"

> which finding itself at the bottom of the kitchen sink,
> late at night, disappeared back down the drain,
> worked its way through the maze of the Cross to
> the roots of the fig tree to climb its trunk and be seen,
> in morning sunlight, motionless on the stump
> of a hacked off branch.

Reportage, you'll say and he denies in the poem a temptation to make this mean. Still, in the writing it has meant, in a different way from (say) Snyder's market particulars, flounder and noodles, people on bicycles, begging bowl.

The fetus in the parlor includes himself, *Baby's Book of Events* (named in the Lascaux poem, quoted as a Joycean list in "Deeds Done and Suffered by Light") the prime physicalizing (textualizing) instance of the Romantic interest in origins, generating instances, that make it a wonder Olson didn't worship prime numbers. It's easy to read Eshleman as imaginative etymology, our cave Fathers as first words, and is this adequate as a response—is response what the poems ask? "I write," Lamb says, "for antiquity." He wants us antlered. Anyway, some books you leaf through (maybe even a Baby's Book) make leafing an imposition. What I *meant* to say before the distracting trappings distracted, was how important, in "River," is his not jacking with that slug the way Longfellow must with gravestones. It does mean, as all of "Visit to Le Tuc" means, that his visioning isn't self-indulgent.

His poems do ask me to adopt his attitude toward his interests, and this shows in his adjectives:

> an increasingly tendrilled fissure,
>
> a massive vulva incised before the gate,
>
> it would be relegated by gradually peaking individuality
> > to the lower body,
>
> awesome, infinite, coiled in hypnosis.

He thinks of adjectives as coiled snakes, perhaps too coarsely imagined as significantly dreaming (that last line ends a poem.) It is like the fairytale poison as opposed to poisoned in poison apple, adjective denoting class.

I write the rest of this in red ink because so many of these poems employ blood in its stringiness and ability to tint, the blood as basic because inner,

> straining the walls
> priming them with menstrual effluvia
>
> All hominids share a scarlet where the dark is

any iron in him implicitly going to platelets. The American sculptors in Rome used drills to make holes, depths in ringlets and those mouths split to glimpsed tongue and teeth. What in Bernini is mannerist live space seeping into stone becomes, for the people Hawthorne met, a fingering of stone with the eye and exercise of techne. It's hard from Lawrence on for blood and thinking snakes, any hysterine red darknesses, not to be this in us. I don't think Jeffers gets out of it. Even late-Greek, you had to *learn* to say Medea. They aren't just there for us, as Jeffers says sunlight on the Pacific is like, so like, Greek islands predating their names.

So, in verse is there a presumption that blood and bile are, as preverbal facts, *in* the poem by owning it, the document in the coffer, *deed* (even) of gift, as Hillman might ask? The assumption that prime substances are interesting *is* the Medusa in these poems, frequent in them, and rightly imagined as in a way stopping language (see Patricia Berry's fine essay on "Stopping" in *Echo's Subtle Body*). Aside from the arrest as at an accident it affects me as if I'd come on a Folly, one of those in the National Trust guidebook. When I try to address or come up to the globality of Eshleman's concern, not in one poem or book in particular but his life as writer-traveler, the question not for him but for me is is this picturesque, a taste for what crumbles from intelligibility, no matter that we've ruins in us to which these speak. Do we paddle in Gothic? Here it's not his vaudeville, dead father and mother speaking from coffins (frightfully Hammer, a detective story says), which I find pious and moving, as Liza Doolittle's dustman father is a Figure that guarantees as if by humor a cleanliness of concern, but the sobriety of his frontal attacks on what you'd think permanently lost even to Frazerian analogizing that convinces me the significances aren't to be proved by my assenting to their effect. It's hard to see this because Eshleman would see their effect *on* me as validation. I mailed him a picture of the Boston Museum's miniature goddess. He wrote back:

> Your marvelous postcard is on my desk. Breastbared snake lady of
> the ovarian lab. Who taught the Minotaur to dance by kissing his
> charred animal muzzle and adopting his pizzle on red Saturdays 12
> times a year. His eyes still have a bit of sorrow and diamond-glint in
> Cocteau's *Beauty and the Beast.* By the time we get to Theseus,
> possession is the thing, and that which does not add up something to be
> squashed instead of inducted.

This in passing in a note. So it's not as if he's putting a mask on
in the poems. He exploits neither of our curiosities (so Alice-like
in "Le Tuc") about origins, and is not—as so much Tennyson and
Arnold seem to be—replacing the father as a project. That's Joyce
again, Hamlet as ghost, and I can't but think Berry's essay on Hamlet
and words, which in its attack on repetition leads into stopping,
applicable though I can't say how. What I lack as a shekinah around
Longfellow's gravestones, and as admission in Jeffers that we *do* owe
the Greeks, clarté, is repaired in Eshleman's going back and back
to the caves; it's not as if he's *done* Les Eyzies. I'm old-fashioned
enough to like poems to be Works, definitive. Eshleman's help me
see them not as stages on life's way, essays, tries (who would want
that, the fruit tree each time inventing the apple) but something
else abandoned to print but not to care. He's not a better poet for
caring for cave art as such. I do think his plastic interests perfectly
served by the bison in Le Tuc *modeled* in wet clay. The limestone
walls with superimposed drawings, sometimes glazed from later
dripping, are wonderful to me but not palimpsests of memory
because they can't be that. For that his Cave Fathers would have to
be in my mind like Dickens characters and they're not. He likes
them most when they are nearly goblins, shadows of dactyloi.

What impresses about them is their imagined rituals are absolutes.
Frazer would class nearly all Haitian rituals as sympathetic magic—
blue meal in bowls or poured in figures as food for the departed. Yet
the decorating aspect dominates and they float free of the classification.
So here, beings between shamans and Quatermass and the Pit are like
slugs so much what they announce that Will, like Occupation, thins
because coagulable to a thing to trace two veins without metaphors of
telegraph, the nerve-nets that infected twenties verse to death. His
anatomy, thank goodness, is not Gray's. I do wish he'd do a book of
poems to be illustrated with line drawings of the skulls, including
Piltdown. During his slide lecture the pointing arm and sleeve would
invade the screen space, bits of figured animal on his lapel, himself a
kind of cave. He said it was like the consciousness of man and so,
lumens behind it, dioptrics, it may have been. It would be wrong to

talk of Eshleman's poems as renderings of his notions, as if the image were all on the screen, when it's the bit of tweed, sartorial inadvertence, that humanizes them so. It's hard to know always, for these sorts of poems, what one is supposed to ignore, a surety which as built into Longfellow's and Jeffers's poems destroys them utterly.

# The Physiognomy of Taste

Anne D. Ferry taught me that unless it was Milton you were to forget
everything you knew about an author. If it was Milton it was all right
to remember. Poems were to make their own way, nothing of height
or eye color or timbre except what of these could be written in. Raised
before I hit college on A. Edward Newton and the old *Atlantic* criticism
which made later personalists look impersonal as partner-wanted ads
this was an odd requirement, but something of it stuck. If Todd Baron
has personal characteristics I haven't a notion what they are. All I know
is what he writes. Sir Thomas Browne is no longer available, though
Geoffrey Keynes prints a lovely picture of his skull. Baron's sentences,
for me, are his face. *Return of the World's* "The Rooms," at the start, is
more a stumbling block than some because of the ways it's always
falling toward intelligibility (returning, I suppose *to* the world, or "of"
as in Attack of the Mole People). Since it's called "Rooms" it starts off
outdoors, a startling first line ("we stuff machines or they stuff us")
modulating, staggered, into a second, "yet coming back to one body"
that may be what the poem or book is saying all the time—I'd say so—
to a third and consequent lines "about" a recognizable—gutter water
from an imagined carwashing, so it's as if we wind from token unintelli-
gibility to the usual platform plum, recognizable to make audiences
ah, that Language verse in decline so predictably provides. What we
get instead, and I wish to stress that this is a real trouble, that one is
in real trouble in Baron's poems, is a baldheaded man supposed or
apparently supposed (or remembered, or intruding as in a dream),
mistaken but only for a second for a guarantee of a kind of continuity
at once subverted for a larger thematic unity, the room as a hole in air,
always upper, in the postwar house with predictable stairwell, what
David Searcy calls an Ozzie and Harriet house. Let me give you part:

> we stuff machines or they stuff us
> yet coming back to one body
> that is really a gutter stream
> from up the same block, some-
> one washing or watering his car
> was bald of course,
> he had no hair & we being right

took what little comfort playing dead
in the upper reaches of a tree,
climbing thru a window to look for
something up there, up &
filled from side to side with music,
inside the room, was always dark, &
everyone's house was like that, no scheme
to the possibility that creation was all matter,
a boat somehow without lake, flying, above us
no part yet to go to, it, being
nothing of the sort, we talk now, later
from an incomplete list brought about by some advent
that hasn't the time to
pluck itself from the book, to focus such
attention of the sound of this pronouncement,
careful in consideration, you might
smash the past with doctrine, making all time
an essay on syntax,
leaning to the remainders, a table, there, . . .

The end is very nice about ("about") evolving toward inhabiting
spaces but not offensively textbook to one in love with Darwin as I am.
The question (as I eat this Blue Cross Blue Shield chili, startlingly sweet
from too much ketchup, effect better managed with coriander), is not,
though it might be, is this a poem about what we all know, distressed
to be trendy as one might be surprised by joy.

First I'm pleased with a diction. Too many poems like these put in
a blender could be rearranged to make soap opera scripts in which (I
like to think) no word must jar, or surprise, or intrigue for what, in
itself, it raises. Everyone's diction is always in danger of wearing white
socks. "we stuff machines or" is a good enough opening, and nothing
like *Tender Buttons'* "Rooms." Whether by the "of course" baldheaded
man we wind into a dream landscape as in "As the Dead Prey Upon
Us," a poem as haunting (for me) as "La Belle Dame Sans Merci"
about being haunted, we're amid (even amid ships) spaces defining
themselves in three dimensions. In the heaven of memory mansions
are, for Todd, rooms, meaningful spaces. He fronts these with the
manner (in the posture) of a man about to say something. The relatively
light timbre of these lines makes to take them as occurring in the
second before speech. Yet the words are chosen with great care, as in
Lewis Carroll, are unhappy replaced by other words.

It's surprising how many -ing endings he gets away with in the
rooms—the page even ends with fencing and barbing—when this is
so almost always a symptom of Norman Rockwell poetique. The odd

indentions, which I've xeroxed so the editor won't have to take them off my computer spacing, are unmachinelike at the start, stuffing us with these lines, so much in appearance as if nearly randomly centered but not (one counts numbers of words per line and things, in case equivalent indentions mean something. They don't). And one isn't stopped; it's what the -ings are for, flicking us with the uncompleted sense from line to line. Nothing that we've not had before, but from the ease of it the effect is lyric, with a kind of brash openness too, as a child expects us to be interested in what's said. The author is also, patently, interested *in* this broken line, discourse thinking itself down the page. No element in it, no half-line, is not like something we've thought ourselves or been vehicle for. Yet there is a press-sure from line to line, and how the lines choose to cut themselves off,

> "see it
> not break, but
>
> see it imagine itself
> breaking."

as he says in another place, not about lines. His carry with them an imagining of fracture.

There are whole pages of short lines that aren't much ("I have emptied/the morning//of multiplicity,//arching us more//on the pillow/towards us.") I have? I have emptied the? His words get less distinguished as he denies himself space to go on, and I'd say his shorter-stanza aphorisms fall toward Zukofsky. Here is a piece of highsounding nonsense reading like *Quartets* Eliot making fun of such things but ending with the genuine and admirable sententiousness Zukofsky gets from playing movement against repeating syllables,

> if, in event a wet season,
> a number of acoustic phases
> indices reason, broken,
> reflecting high decision,
> regarded to discarded sentences,
> approximated from the
> cause diverted,
> fully seeded,
> all use evaded,
> appearing ceases.

Still I prefer his raddled left margins by which, hammered into the world somewhere, he's a peg for a bit of snail shell or bird dung to come on, happen to cling to—

> try to remember a thing, or
> a thing doesn't remember me,
> walks & talks & tries to,
> air not clean enough, stance
> really a sufferage worked by nature
> to be still-born
> visible to emit
> illuminating rays
> to let the light through,
> a solid secondary root, lawn or grass
> or front lawn gets cut every week,
> but wood softens, is soft, what
> need of sounds
> to reciprocate,

as if the poem is a fence around the poet. The facing page has a lovely book-reviewish poem beginning "page a cipher word or script" about the reader's consciousness as "like" the writer's, corroding as he goes the bad (too purely conventional) writing he describes, to end prettily with

> lines fade as
> who is sung clings to the possibility
> of particulars also.

He can be playful without being silly or foolishly arch, as in this wee anthologizable (another self-contained one),

> an edible landscape
> near the front of the drawer
> the cassette
> slips in.

These lines know other lines exist, that poems in clumps whisper on, the sounds they make moulting. There are zombie poems, duppies, built as if on the remembered vein structure of leaves fallen to lace. The best of them incorporate a sound made about intent. Baron's too good for this, his poems too interesting in progress, as they go, but he does end the book with a burning-deck recitation, kind of dauntless, that begs to end a review so I forgo it (Baron is unusual for a Language poet in that he can, for instance, spell the word "forgo.") What I'd rather observe is that after disorienting you absolutely by the mirror sculpture we all know how to do (so all that's left is to make it pretty) he can end any old time with a loveliness like this:

two or three stories at once,
then, in the passing phrase,
is it who or whom, made-up
in the upper reaches of speech
where it rains & doesn't rain,
this room and those rooms,
alive
to a particular place,
on the edge of a black and white set,
caught by a hook, going away
as syntax does not know
the words are not mine but written,
the words are not words, but lines.

There's a kind of dogged removal one can do (and I've done myself) with "not," like the dissolving hypotheticals in some Ashbery, that makes it awfully hard to keep a reader well disposed toward lines like these. I don't say it's our job to hold a reader's attention, or conciliate if it means decorating a poem with generica. I'd say rather Baron's lines are a lie; his syntax knows it's written and his words that they are lines, make lines. The scenes by him, caught by hooks, don't quite succeed themselves like slides, remembered as if heard, having been heard, and if his models for meaning are not very interesting his analogies are his life's, so genuine it's as well they're private. I could wish he (and maybe only he) would write his poems two ways, one rather placidly disclosing his hideous occasions. These skeleton confessions are like Mayan picturebooks, what is that man doing with that knife. . . . It would be, for one who never meets authors, like having the undistinguished dustjacket photo, usually taken by a loved one, to go on. How blank they are, as if the writer's dead, no one about whom one'd care. But it's something that I'd like Todd ("t b" in the title poem for which I do not care) to write paired poems to make him less an effigy, less the writer of these. A nervousness in these should be buried in mud, not "anchored in reality" at all, just vandalized a little.

# Letter to Michael Franco

Dear Michael,

This is very nice and very sad. Now do (again) write the thing, preferably drily. I don't much mind it being wet, or slippery, or treacherously refractive. But you do think still you can write about all of it at once while looking at all of it at once, and you will, but right now you should write about all of it at once while looking at some of it.

You feel so deeply you think it's there. For instance—Oedipus's eyes—reading those lines even after I talked to you I *still* never see them as eyes discarded, on the ground, but as (say) trick opaque contact lenses, an actor's device to look like a sandblasted Greek statue, makeup as referential (very end of *The Man with X-Ray Eyes,* Ray Milland's opaque red under the lids, then black).

Is it, for example, all right to break a line there because your spirit breaks there, or is that augmenting a weakness? The line-break as catch in the throat is *extremely* difficult, and yet you're always doing it. It's as if, very sensitive, you can feel your reaction *to* what you're writing about coming on (from a distance) and, beginning to quiver, break the line there.

Personally I don't think anyone as tall as you should do that.

And, this verse explains:

> laughter and silence
> vaporous conclusions of the mind's
> outpouring of
> general loneliness that this
> continual procession past
> each particular
>     other
>     is

If you don't mind, look what energy "vaporous" and "continual" drain by looking so much like bad writing, even if they're *exactly what you meant.* Intending is not a defense.

And then it's hard to end a line, and a verse bloc, and an indented verse bloc, with "is" without looking like a cufflink on Olson's shirt. This is or may be partly your subject, but I feel reading it your "is"

**118**

hasn't earned its difference. And this is an investigation—you commit all the procedural-cue signalings—

"Let me quote—as a marginal illustration—from..."

"OK—so this then as a 'preface'—a key to guide..."

"The first,"

"To put it simply,"

"These then are not..."

"The question then is..."

"that only this true darkness
can expose"

"Forced    we think
   at our will's command

we are
no more than
the instrument of these bare branches"

—(which is to say, we think obediently, a more than possible construction but since the next lines take the *form of* a cliché you get, not ruin'd choirs or In cold hell, in thicket but humor of a Robert Benchley sort.)

As didactic verse I prefer Pound's

the white house
the white house

it ain't
no light
house

or however he broke the lines.

Your serious, sober, what-life-is-like-made-sense-of lines *plonk* when better they should lurch and clank. As you say you like verse to find out things, investigate *as* it goes. I'm not sure your didactic lines have the energy (yet) to grab evocative enough words *and* break the lines right, while thinking (which is an effort), and I know it's odd, letting rhythm, rate and line-breaks help determine the thought *while* disposing of these things a little *as if* they are taste matters, in their way as "separate" from thinking as rhyme, no more no less. Buy your meat and meal in Georgia.

Oh Michael you have to cut it all (not this, necessarily, but you know everything you write that's savable has as if been thrown away at least once. I just came on this in "Roastbeef," *it is so easy to exchange meaning, it is so easy to see the difference.* That line (in 1911) ruins all simple transpositional Language writing, dismisses it as not interesting enough because too transparent in its principle, its manner of proceeding, and only then in its effect.

How your mouth says vowels and consonants is so entertaining,

> the water's     still
> surface
> beneath this rock
> is moving
> small brown bird
> yellow tipped wings
>        butterfly
> ants        gnats
> wind
> and breath
>        swell        echoing
> all
> I        am
> still
> here
> fingers pusht into the
> deep rock-moss
>
> listening

I always like it that you're tactile, and that sounds crash into you, are foreign rather than expected—even speech. Your verse can barely manage

> Drive, he
> sd

without a jar. Good. But when you talk about how common things are displayed (disposed) about you, the sense of what is foreign (not your body) vanishes, so in an odd way it doesn't *matter* what, in your descriptions, happens to be around you. It's all really you. I grieve with your grief in these, sky in trees, and wish you could grieve more *for* the sky than you do, though this is medieval habit, with me. A vigorous sense that all creatures and contexts made of them are in the same boat. Gilson says it's from *Genesis,* a strong and ungreek sense that anything could as easily not be. Heidegger asks why is there anything rather than nothing (he was an altarboy. That's what it does to you.) So

> along the river-bank
> under trees
> that are
> sky

all these are horribly in question, jeopard, hence hardly useful as anchors to judge a change in your life. The pastoral convention that when the shepherd dies trees weep, "for Lycidas, that he is dead" becomes medieval and hence no longer sentimental—of course the world alters. So this needs rendering in the line, and a pity for sky and tree (trees being sky, as a reflecting lake in Wordworth busies itself being mountain), and I bet you say (around now) it's there. Nothing sillier than prescribing a current regimen.

Current, that which flows. Is it with your mood, or the order you think of things *and* your foreseeing, almost predicting, what you'll think about next making a needle-quiver you then record, that's verse thinking for you? How do the words, nestling, move? Thought (I notice) is not always friendly. Yours can be too summer-breezy to make the forthright invest-igative-manner delivery sensible. Lecturing while sauntering.

So what's a field for you or me except firstly a situation, not necessar-ily perceived distinctly but always (from principle) taken account of. Yours is often visual, a description of room and kettle before the poem starts, obviously intending itself as part of what's then said. But your housescapes are usually placid (I'd say from the verbs), and what I notice for me is that surroundings are always thinking/working exactly as hard as I am, by a kind of good fortune—so it's hard or impossible for me to contrast a landscape to what's in me. Probably *Lucy Church Amiably* investigates all that, how sky is and is not one below it, the senses of "in."

I notice that everything needs investigation.

How fortunate Olson's in thicket and Dante in a wood (ya selva oscura) when they need it, rather than a desert or Longfellow's formal garden. So they have to handle that, the *contingent* nature of the ambient metaphor, that the given gives, and needn't. Everything matters but isn't honor-bound to, and what you ignore matters too which is why, throwing seven stones for geomancy, there's an eighth formally unused.

Now here you are in a batch of lines, thin column with odd inden-tions—why is this going on, the philosopher asks. G. E. Moore says my *hand,* I know it's really *there.* Wittgenstein devastates him by asking who but a philosopher would say this? (What possessed him.) Who but a poet would, finding himself on a page, write so oddly. Olson indent-ing stanzas and so on, scoring like and unlike Pound, takes advantage of the oddity by leaning on it, calling attention to it, and making his intent the reason for it. Then, he's talking out of himself (his kitchen, its windows facing on his first view of the sea, etc.), histories. How can you doing this make so much of "the unrealized promise of light" (I couldn't make a thing of it myself.) The light promises because it is a presence, and you can, in theory, given light like other light in different circumstances take it as having gone back on a promise (Dante, on Purgatory shore, dragged back to hell by winged apes in bellboy caps). But really light bends to the situation, like getting through the glass flowers in Peabody. It feels it isn't easy. Light is *wary*.

So you don't want to write of it as unconscious, inadvertent, and for this reason you keep it separate from "slow eyes . . . rising so dark/in the half-light" so the light won't be too obedient, honor-bound to greet. There's choice on both sides. Then you observe that while an aubade is two elements (her eyes and dawn) there are really many, and you mustn't let a pair of nouns dictate all your verbs. Cézanne putting two, three, five marks on a blank canvas, distinct, couldn't they say but make them beautiful, breathtaking, all knowing (like his apples, jars) each, at that level too.

So that's a *test* of field, how small a fraction of the poem says all of it. Olson sensibly wanted all syllables to, not so much "and thus their own hell and paradise" but certainly

> He shall step, he
> will shape, he
> is already also
> moving off
> > into the soil, on to his own bones
> he will cross
> > (there is always a field,
> > for the strong there is always
> > an alternative)
> > > But a field
> > is not a choice, is
> > as dangerous as a prayer, as a death, as any
> > misleading, lady

and these are still too commonplace except in their commas and then their line-breaks, and what's *revolutionary* is the relation of their commas to the line-breaks. Rough thinking in verse should be revolutionary like dabs of "color," so much their pattern first, in a building canvas.

You can almost see that Olson knows his words aren't *quite* interesting enough (perhaps because the sense takes his attention and thinking to himself he thinks in little words, how, always, there is, as dangerous as, so you get all his phrases bracketing as lines with is and as, all the dodges he worked like a union organizer so they'll pull together instead of, as you'd think, dissipate energy.

>           for the strong there is always
>           an alternative)

is a rhythm he's used before, come down hard on, so look at him pull
out of it by continuing it, simply keep the rate moving:

>               for the strong there is always
>               an alternative)
>                           But a field
>                       is not a choice, is

He shows you the alternative to settling into a line rhythmically definitive. How interesting that he takes a field as dangerous because takable
as given—not as given but as takable as given. He likes it cosmically
there, like a dare (bad weather to a dory, freeze your hands, on the
oars). And his line-ends so cat-footed, so finicky, gain energy *not*
merely from saying I am subtle as Scotus or Hugh of St. Victor. But he
does say, here, if there is a field then you can always move. The
motion in his verse comes from the verse, as a whole, defining itself as
inhabiting what, even if pure despair, *contains points.*

The assumption is like the sound in Antarctic exploration journals,
that motion could occur. I do like it for verse on a page to have this
kind of circumspection, and it may be why I prefer my own lines a
little tightly set. Keep the white space at bay. Verse is a tent.

Let us, in any given line, sound as if we are chewing it over and
over. Eskimos made a ridge at the crest of the skull from chewing
leather to make it soft. It anchors muscle. That's no metaphor for
making verse, but probably *within* the gang who think they're compos-
ing by field you can distinguish those pushing or pulling off an imagined fixity (if only the field itself) and those happy to float (in local
effects). Even a planet's gravity well is more than a local effect, though
it registers as a local disturbance (installs a little physics). Anyone can
always say to anyone "You're not *local* enough," as you could accuse
St. Francis of insufficient humility and he'd agree. No one knows where
he is. David Searcy thinks all the time about location.

So, as if you are in a religion, you find yourself in a field you're
somehow in complicity with, though this can sound like the silliest
Stoicism or Est. Active and passive can be as fake as the woman's eyes
and dawn as an exhaustive list. In ways the point of attention is that
what is attended to is all there is, and in that sense an act of attention is
a poem. Coleridge agreed with Kant that any commonplace perceptual
manifold is a bleeding corpse transfixed with imagination. The imagination chews its dogs while snow falls.

So, in your back garden, you and Andrea sympathetic when we come over to cheer you, a bright penny on mossy dirt between flagstones is a littler decoration, not to be picked up. Its value is almost as not picked up though it's hard to hold to this without sentimentality. "Don't cut them, I pleaded." (Remember "The Act" by William Carlos Williams?)

> Agh, we were all beautiful once, she
>            said,
> and cut them and gave them to me
>            in my hand.

That's breaking through a field, and changing the given by deed of gift. Williams and his grandmother quarrel about what constitutes a field. The field contains notions of suitable comportment. Any field does. I think it's wise now, especially in the face of the magazine poem selling a sensibility, for a poem's assumptions about comportment inside itself to be at risk. The writer must assume a poem can hurt back.

Yet the metaphor that the field *is* experience, that to go afield is to be abroad, hurts too.

> What wine does one drink?
> What bread does one eat?

What air does one breathe, in a poem that's a field, how take its arctic temperature? Can we know, even (not just gauge but know) if Thomas's "Over Sir John's hill" is a tried parody of Hopkins (which it is if we skim a few lines, and always in some typefaces) or look at all of it as a whole poem among poems, say in the P.E.N. anthology where it's better by miles than anything else.

I'd like to see a whole poem about inclining and inclination. You could call its book *Gradient*. I don't care if the little measuring nicks in Descartes's axes go all tattered, become emblems of measurement. There's a faith that a thing can be done or can be going on I like to see in a poem. It's wrong to say there'd be no depression if everyone kept a faith in banks, Frank Capra economics. Can we say "Anyone can fail" without complicity in failure? Dig graves denying death? A poem is a field *rather than* a room so that reading may be a jaunt. The poem collects little attentions, or organizes a tour, or drowns you in rhythm. To say a poem is a field reduces the family likeness almost to zero. What makes them readable beyond a common language is a venturesome generosity in the writer. It's the readable poems, that leap out of the envelope or magazine already reading themselves that are difficult, like eating a Whopper with connoisseurship.

*Gerald Burns* was an old-fashioned (*Amenities of Book-Collecting*) Johnsonian before he became a Stein scholar, and read prose at Harvard in order to write poetry. He has been guest lecturer at Simon Fraser University, poet in residence at the University of Millersville, and a frequent contributor of texts and critiques to publications grounded in Language. Since 1969 he has been engaged in a XII-book long poem, *The Myth of Accidence,* of which the first eight sections have been published. In 1985 he was awarded an NEA Creative Writing Fellowship for poetry.